_$ 29.00_

**New Directions for
Child and Adolescent
Development**

Reed W. Larson
Lene Arnett Jensen
EDITORS-IN-CHIEF

William Damon
FOUNDING EDITOR

Attachment in Adolescence: Reflections and New Angles

Miri Scharf
Ofra Mayseless
EDITORS

Number 117 • Fall 2007
Jossey-Bass
San Francisco

ATTACHMENT IN ADOLESCENCE: REFLECTIONS AND NEW ANGLES
Miri Scharf, Ofra Mayseless (eds.)
New Directions for Child and Adolescent Development, no. 117
Reed W. Larson, Lene Arnett Jensen, Editors-in-Chief

Microfilm copies of issues and articles are available in 16mm and 35mm, as well as microfiche in 105mm, through University Microfilms, Inc., 300 North Zeeb Road, Ann Arbor, Michigan 48106-1346.

ISSN 1520-3247   electronic ISSN 1534-8687

NEW DIRECTIONS FOR CHILD AND ADOLESCENT DEVELOPMENT is part of The Jossey-Bass Education Series and is published quarterly by Wiley Subscription Services, Inc., a Wiley company, at Jossey-Bass, 989 Market Street, San Francisco, California 94103-1741. Periodicals postage paid at San Francisco, California, and at additional mailing offices. Postmaster: Send address changes to New Directions for Child and Adolescent Development, Jossey-Bass, 989 Market Street, San Francisco, CA 94103-1741.

New Directions for Child and Adolescent Development is indexed in Cambridge Scientific Abstracts (CSA/CIG), CHID: Combined Health Information Database (NIH), Contents Pages in Education (T&F), Current Abstracts (EBSCO), Educational Research Abstracts Online (T&F), ERIC Database (Education Resources Information Center), Index Medicus/MEDLINE/PubMed (NLM), Linguistics & Language Behavior Abstracts (CSA/CIG), Psychological Abstracts/PsycINFO (APA), Social Services Abstracts (CSA/CIG), SocINDEX (EBSCO), and Sociological Abstracts (CSA/CIG).

SUBSCRIPTION rates: For the U.S., $85 for individuals and $258 for institutions. Please see ordering information page at end of journal.

EDITORIAL CORRESPONDENCE should be e-mailed to the editors-in-chief: Reed W. Larson (larsonr@uiuc.edu) and Lene Arnett Jensen (ljensen@clarku.edu).

Jossey-Bass Web address: www.josseybass.com

Contents

1

Intriguing issues pertaining to normative changes in attachment in adolescence are addressed, integrating psychoanalytical thinking, developmental and attachment theory, and research.

Putting Eggs in More Than One Basket: A New Look at Developmental Processes of Attachment in Adolescence

Miri Scharf, Ofra Mayseless

"In some ways we know a great deal about attachment in adolescence, yet in other respects we know disconcertingly little. . . . Attempts to assess attachment in adolescence inevitably must confront the questions of what attachment becomes and what function it serves during this stage of the lifespan" (Allen & Land, 1999, p. 331). This concluding remark of the intgrative chapter on attachment in adolescence in the *Handbook of Attachment* is the opening point of this chapter and volume.

In recent years the number of empirical studies examining attachment in adolescence has grown. Most of the research has focused on individual differences in attachment security. This chapter seeks to extend previous research and theorizing on attachment in adolescence by elaborating on what might be considered the normative, universal developmental processes of the behavioral system of attachment during adolescence. To this end we use the notion of developmental tasks, which have been defined as socially, psychologically, and biologically determined activities or goals that individuals are expected to accomplish at certain ages or stages of life. The content and timing of such tasks are expected to be a function of biological capabilities and socially constructed norms and expectations (Schulenberg, Bryant, & O'Malley, 2004). We discuss four developmental tasks that adolescents

NEW DIRECTIONS FOR CHILD AND ADOLESCENT DEVELOPMENT, no. 117, Fall 2007   © Wiley Periodicals, Inc.
Published online in Wiley InterScience (www.interscience.wiley.com) • DOI: 10.1002/cd.191

commonly face concerning expected changes in the structure and operation of their attachment behavioral system: changes in the way attachment is expressed, changes in the targets of attachment behaviors, changes in the composition and structure of network of attachment figures, and changes in attachment internalized models.

We follow the ideas set forth by Bowlby and later developed by Ainsworth and adopt the ethological and evolutionary perspectives regarding the primacy, universality, and biological basis of attachment. We also build on a large group of researchers and scholars who have suggested various ideas and models. We further rely on two additional bodies of research: the research literature on developmental changes in adolescence and psychoanalytically oriented conceptualizations and observations. Our analysis is not intended to be a state-of-the-art review but as a somewhat speculative, and we hope challenging proposal that raises new research questions and opens up fruitful arenas for research. We address intriguing issues pertaining to normative changes in attachment in adolescence:

1. *Turning away from parents.* How can we explain the seemingly universal tendency of adolescents (even those who enjoy secure relationships with their parents) to distance themselves from their parents, and even deliberately refrain from turning to them in times of distress?
2. *Turning to others (not parents).* Why do we see strong investment in relations with peers that seem to acquire partial properties of attachment relationships? Are these really attachment relationships? How can we explain other emotional and social investments characteristic of this period, in the self and in distant others?
3. *Forming pair-bonds.* Where does all this lead? Is the end point of this ontogenetic developmental trajectory the creation of an attachment pair-bond with a sexual mate that assumes primacy in the attachment hierarchy?
4. *Convergence and diversity in working models of attachment.* How can we explain the convergence of one overarching style or state of mind coexisting with many different, alternative and competing submodels?
5. *Individual differences.* How do adolescents with different attachment models navigate the developmental tasks of attachment in adolescence?

Turning Away from Parents

There are clear indications in the developmental literature that in adolescence, the reliance on parents as exclusive attachment figures decreases (Allen & Land, 1999). Adolescents spend less time with parents and family and more time with peers (Larson, Richards, Moneta, Holmbeck, & Duckett, 1996; Youniss & Smollar, 1989). There is a decline in shared activities and in the extent of physical affection between adolescents and parents (Conger & Ge, 1999; Salt, 1991) and an increased need for privacy (Josselson, 1980; Steinberg & Silk, 2002).

NEW DIRECTIONS FOR CHILD AND ADOLESCENT DEVELOPMENT • DOI: 10.1002/cd

Furthermore, bickering and disagreements over everyday issues characterize parent-adolescent relationships, particularly during early adolescence (Collins & Laursen, 2004). Although conflicts normally provide adolescents with arenas for improving negotiation skills, conflicts with parents during adolescence are generally resolved through disengagement or giving in to parents. Conflict frequency peaks in early adolescence, while conflict intensity increases from early to middle adolescence (Collins & Steinberg, 2006).

Other indications of this distancing between adolescents and parents were found in studies that specifically examined attachment processes. For example, Ammaniti, van IJzendoorn, Speranza, and Tambelli (2000) followed participants from ages ten to fourteen using the Adult Attachment Interview (AAI). With age, the adolescents increased their tendencies of derogation of parents and lack of recall, and they perceived their parents as more rejecting. Similarly, in Scharf (2001) and in Scharf, Mayseless, and Kivenson-Baron (2004), many of the adolescents categorized as autonomous in the AAI were characterized by restriction in expression of attachment sentiments even when talking coherently about their relationships.

In line with this tendency of distancing, Hazan, Hutt, Sturgeon, and Bricker (1991), who asked children and adolescents to name people they would choose for different attachment functions, found that at age seventeen, 75 percent preferred peers to parents in the functions of proximity seeking and separation protest. Even in the function of secure base, parents were only somewhat favored over peers (55 percent versus 45 percent).

How do we account for these processes? According to psychoanalytical thinking (Freud, 1958), the physical changes of puberty play a central role in triggering parent-adolescent distancing. The reawakening of oedipal emotions and sexual drives is expressed in internal conflicts between the id and the superego, and externally in bickering and distancing between adolescents and their parents. It has been argued that emotional detachment from parents is needed to allow investment in extrafamilial relationships.

From a sociobiological viewpoint (Steinberg, 1990), bickering between parents and adolescents has been interpreted as ensuring that adolescents will spend time away from their families. This behavior serves to prevent incest and guarantee investment in relationships with nonkin. Such distancing between youngsters and parents is almost universally observed in non-human primates, and it serves to minimize inbreeding and enhance reproductive fitness. This need is exacerbated by psychosocial historical changes. Over the past century, the amount of time that physically mature youngsters and their parents live in close contact has increased, thus threatening the genetic integrity of the species and enhancing the need to actively use various means to distance from parents (Steinberg, 1987).

The distancing and the weakening of emotional investment in parents may serve yet another evolutionary purpose: promoting self-reliance and individuation. Enduring dependency on parents might jeopardize youngsters in the long run. To increase survival fitness, the young need to be self-reliant and fend for themselves. Adolescents should be prepared to function independently to ensure their survival should their parents not be around, a likely occurrence. These processes refer to psychological and instrumental separation from the actual parent, expressed in the need to obtain and manifest to oneself and to others that one has the capacity to solve problems and face challenging and stressful situations by oneself and survive. This demand is prominent in many rites of passage in various cultures (Ford & Beach, 1951).

The processes of establishing self-reliance involve a less overt part too: individuation from the introjected parent of infancy (Josselson, 1980). Josselson (1980, p. 193) provides a compelling description:

> In large part, the early adolescent attempts to feel separate and distinct from his parents by finding ways of irritating them. This is a way of flexing the will, of proving to oneself that one is taken seriously as a separate person. . . . In order to deal more effectively with the introjects, the adolescent may project them back into the reality parents and, for example, fly into a rage when his mother asks, where are you going? For a moment the reality mother is experienced as controlling, over powerful mother of early childhood. This interaction, although it takes place in reality, has its meaning vis-à-vis the internal world.

The actual separation and the disengagement from internalized models reflect the individuation process (Blos, 1962). In the words of Blos (1967, p. 168), "Individuation implies that the growing person takes increasing responsibility for what he does and what he is, rather than depositing this responsibility on the shoulders of those under whose influence and tutelage he has grown up."

Frequently adolescents were described as striving for such autonomy and self-reliance, while parents were described as having difficulties in letting go and trying to preserve the dependencies of their offspring (Stierlin, 1981). From the perspective of attachment theory, there is no reason to assume that the developmental tasks of parents and adolescents are incompatible. On the contrary, from a parental perspective, there is an evolutionary advantage for raising an autonomous offspring who can function and survive on his or her own (Youniss & Smollar 1989). Only in cases where relationships are entangled and insecure would we expect considerable difficulties.

The processes of distancing and weakening of emotional investment and dependency on parents are reminiscent of the process described in psychoanalytical writings as *decathexis* (Rycroft, 1995). *Cathexis* represents the binding of emotional feeling and significance to an idea or a person. *Decathexis* refers to unbinding of interest, attention, emotional involvement, or energy (libido) from one person or issue so that it can be reinvested in oneself or in another person or area. We suggest that a process reminiscent of decathexis occurs in adolescence and can be construed as a developmental task. This process involves reducing emotional investment in parents and refocusing and redirecting some of this investment to relationships with peers or nonfamily members.

Interestingly these processes of individuation and distancing seem to be accompanied by connectedness with parents (Youniss & Smollar, 1989; Blos, 1967). Although adolescents deidealize their parents and at times avoid their parents, particularly when they are stressed (Allen & Land, 1999), this temporary distancing does not imply cessation of attachment to parents (Ainsworth, 1989). In general most adolescents enjoy warm and close relationships with their parents, need their validation and respect, consult with them, and turn to them when distressed (Steinberg, 1990), and most adults continue to have meaningful and close relationships with their parents (Zarit & Eggebeen, 2002).

Thus, adolescents appear to invest emotionally less in their relationships with parents, so that these relationships "penetrate fewer aspects of their lives than they did before" (Ainsworth, 1989, p. 36). They further appear to redefine the quality of the relationship with their parents as more equal and mutual, but they do not relinquish their parents as attachment figures. Unlike most primates, which leave their parents for good following puberty (Fraley, Brumbaugh, & Marks, 2005) and thus can and should disengage completely from their parents, this is not the normative trajectory of attachment relationships for humans. After adolescents succeed in decreasing emotional investment in parents, succeed in forming relationships outside the family of origin, and prove to themselves that they can manage and function independently, they seem willing and able to rely on their parents once more. As a result, adolescence does not involve permanently severing ties with parents, but rather decreasing their importance and intensity. The extent to which this importance and intensity decrease, as well as the extent to which late adolescents or young adults go back to relying on their parents, is quite varied. It depends on individual differences but is also considerably influenced by the cultural, ecological, and historical context (Belsky, 1999; Scharf & Mayseless, 2004).

Turning to Others

The literature on relationships with peers in adolescence underscores their importance and unique role. Empirical research suggests that during adolescence, perception of parents as the primary sources of support declines, and perceived support from friends increases (Hazan & Zeifman, 1994; Collins & Steinberg, 2006). Furthermore, friends are perceived as providing similar (Scholte, Van Lieshout, & Van Aken, 2001) or even greater support than parents do (Furman & Buhrmester, 1992). At least some adolescent friendships are characterized by loyalty, intimacy, and disclosure; hence, they evince some of the characteristics of attachment relationships (Furman & Buhrmester, 1992).

NEW DIRECTIONS FOR CHILD AND ADOLESCENT DEVELOPMENT • DOI: 10.1002/cd

In adolescence, peers play a much larger role in providing felt security in times of need and in helping to regulate distress in alarming and fear-inducing situations. Furthermore, proximity seeking and separation distress, which help maintain the availability and exclusivity of the specific relationship with a preferred peer, are observed. In addition, adolescents feel more secure and confident to explore the world, in particular the interpersonal world of sexual relationships in the company and proximity of a good friend.

Yet the commitment and strong emotional investment that include a sense of being able to trust the other forever and for "real" survival issues, which characterize most relationships with parents, are in most cases lacking in relationships with peers. There is substantial instability in friendships during adolescence (Hardy, Bukowski, & Sippola, 2002). Moreover, the belief that most adolescents have a special and exclusive close friendship in which attachment qualities are common is not necessarily true and should be examined more systematically. Probably most adolescents have a preferred peer; however, these relationships are not always mutual and not necessarily intensive in nature (Brown & Klute, 2003).

Consistent with these findings, Ainsworth (1989) argued that some friendships have an attachment component and some, but not all, constitute enduring affectional bonds. However, she suggests that whereas close friends may drift apart as their interests change and their friendship becomes less satisfying, bonds with kin tend to be more persistent, even if more ambivalent. The explanation offered is rooted in evolution and notions of the importance of gene survival (Ainsworth, 1989). Whereas stable relationships with kin serve a gene survival function, those with friends do not. Together the lack of long-term commitment in most friendships, as well as their negotiable and transitory nature, and the lack of mourning reactions to termination of most friendships, raise doubts about the extent to which most friendships are real attachment bonds.

What is the meaning and significance of these processes in terms of normative and ontogenetic development of attachment in adolescence? First, investing emotionally in friendships and relying on peers' support allows the adolescent to distance and lessen investment in relationships with parents and find another interpersonal avenue in which to monitor and regulate his or her distress feelings.

Second, experiencing some attachment functions in relationships with peers paves the way to learning more mutual and egalitarian attachment relationships in which both parties provide and receive care and protection. Reciprocal relationships are essential for mating and survival, and they promote the development of adult-like attachment relationships (Allen & Land, 1999), as well as caregiving capacities. The relationships with peers enable practicing and scaffolding and lay the foundation for developing future mature romantic relationships. Thus, relationships with peers may be seen as the training ground for the formation of egalitarian attachment relationships, which cannot in principle be learned within the hierarchical attachment relationships with parents.

Third, the incorporation into one's attachment network of new and often diverse figures with whom adolescents practice attachment behaviors and sentiments enables much higher flexibility in times of stress. Adults in the making who need more autonomy and space might find it wiser to distribute the emotional investment across several figures. Instead of a moderately centralized investment that characterizes the attachment relationship and attachment network in infancy and childhood, adolescents spread their now-freed emotional investments in relationships among several figures. In such diversification, the availability of one figure is less important if other figures are around. Furthermore, adolescents might not yet be mature enough to make a final choice of a full-fledged attachment figure with long-term commitment. Therefore, in such an unstable context, it is better to decentralize emotional investments.

This diversification takes several interesting forms, all discussed (albeit not in an attachment context) in the developmental research on adolescence. For example, the tendency to diversify and decentralize emotional investments might explain adolescents' affiliation with clique members (Brown, 2004) and the importance of friends for the felt security of the adolescent. Furthermore, adolescents might sometimes develop secondary or supplementary attachments to mentors, instructors, and other less authoritative adult figures. These relationships may differ from primary attachments in their lower levels of commitment, yet they may serve several attachment functions, in particular, assistance in regulating negative emotions and the provision of a secure base from which to explore (Ainsworth, 1989).

Even distant or symbolic relationships with idols may serve some of the functions of diversification of emotional investment. The deidealization of parents paves the way for idealization of such figures (Giles & Maltby, 2004). In these actual or symbolic relationships, adolescents are able to learn through emulating new and diverse models of being and succeeding in life. Highlighting the attachment aspect in such symbolic relationships, scholars have suggested that strong "relationships" with celebrities might develop during times of stress or for individuals with less positive peer relationships (Giles & Maltby, 2004). Specifically, when adolescents do not want to, or cannot, rely on parents, or when reliance on peers is partly compromised, turning to idols even in a symbolic way may serve the regulation of self-worth and emotional distress. The transitory role of such emotional investments is nicely illustrated in the words of Blos (1967, pp. 166–167): "It should not surprise us that the bedroom walls, plastered with the collective idols, become bare as soon as object libido is engaged in genuine relationships. Then, the pictorial flock of transient gods and goddesses is rendered dispensable almost overnight."

Another observed propensity related to the decathexis process and diversification in the service of higher self-sufficiency is adolescents' heightened investment in the self, which is expressed in intensive self-absorption. As Blos (1967, p. 173) pointed out, "We observe in adolescence that object libido—in various degrees, to be sure—is withdrawn from outer and inner objects and is converted into narcissistic libido by being deflected onto the self. This shift from object to self results in the proverbial self-centeredness and self absorption of the adolescent who fancies himself to be independent from the love and hate objects of his childhood." This investment in the self might be expressed in the phenomenon of the imaginary audience, adolescents' tendency to see themselves at the center of others' attention, and in the personal fable phenomenon: adolescents' belief in their uniqueness, invulnerability, and omnipotence. These experiences too facilitate the individuation process in that they allow the decrease in emotional investment in parents (Lapsley, 1993). Belief in the imaginary audience makes possible continuing connectedness, while the personal fable facilitates the strivings for increased uniqueness and separateness.

In sum, the weakening of investment in parents does not normatively lead to investment in peers as full-blown attachment figures. Rather it appears to lead to a diversification of emotional investment to various sources: the self as source of security, relationships with friends with some attachment properties, actual or symbolic relationships with nonparental adults such as a coach or an idol, and relationships with romantic partners. These processes are construed here as developmental tasks of adolescence with regard to the attachment system.

Forming Pair-Bonds

From research conducted mostly in Western and industrialized cultures (Collins & Steinberg, 2006), it is quite clear that in adolescence, relationships with romantic partners change considerably with age in terms of frequency, importance, and quality. For example, in a representative sample in the United States, about 25 percent of twelve year olds reported having had a "special romantic relationship" in the previous eighteen months; these numbers increased to about 50 percent in fifteen year olds and to 70 percent by age eighteen (Carver, Joyner, & Udry, 2003). By age seventeen to eighteen, 60 percent reported being in a relationship that persisted eleven months or more. Thus, stable romantic relationships become prevalent only in late adolescence.

Furthermore, the evidence so far indicates that early adolescents perceive their romantic relations in an idealized and stereotypical way, tend to choose partners mostly following expectations of their social networks and in the service of status attainment, and emphasize superficial features of potential partners such as fashionable clothes (Zani, 1993). Thus, needs for status attainment, sexual experimentation, and recreation reflecting the affiliative and sexual and reproduction behavioral systems are the most salient in romantic relationships in early adolescence (Furman & Wehner, 1997;

NEW DIRECTIONS FOR CHILD AND ADOLESCENT DEVELOPMENT • DOI: 10.1002/cd

Shulman & Scharf, 2000). During late adolescence and early adulthood, the attachment and caregiving systems become more prominent in romantic relationships. Older adolescents tend to choose romantic partners based on intimacy and compatibility (Zani, 1993), and romantic relationships begin to fulfill needs for support and caregiving (Furman & Wehner 1997; Scharf & Mayseless, 2001).

Ainsworth (1989) argued that "the hormonal, neurophysiological, and cognitive changes lead the young person to begin a search for a partnership with an age peer, usually of the opposite sex—a relationship in which the reproductive and caregiving systems, as well as the attachment system, are involved" (p. 710). In line with this depiction, attachment researchers have argued that adolescence and young adulthood involve a transfer of attachment functions from parents to peers, and eventually to a romantic partner. Some scholars (Hazan & Zeifman, 1994) have suggested a gradual transfer that starts with changes in the figures to whom proximity maintenance and separation distress are directed, continues with changes in the safe haven function (to whom do individuals turn when they are distressed), and is finalized with changes in the secure base function (the person whose availability allows individuals to feel bolder to explore the world). This transfer is mostly to peers, though other adult figures may also be involved.

In the previous section we suggested that although reorienting emotional investment toward friends serves attachment functions, relationships with them normatively do not replace parents and in most cases do not become full-fledged committed attachment bonds. These relationships might serve as a transitory stage in the process of transfer of attachment and emotional investment from parents to a romantic partner. According to this view, the end point of the developmental trajectory of the attachment behavioral system is the creation of a full-fledged committed attachment pair-bond with a sexual mate who replaces the primary caregivers, mostly parents, at the head of the attachment hierarchy.

What is the current evidence regarding the place of romantic relationships as attachment bonds in adolescence? Do they indeed function as attachment relationships, or at least acquire attachment functions? And do they normatively replace parents as primary attachment figures?

The evidence so far seems to suggest that this trajectory is apparent in some individuals and in some cultures but is not universal; in particular, it is far less universal than the attachment to a caregiver in infancy that characterizes primates and even mammals. Although a discussion of this perspective would direct us to consider attachment processes in adulthood, knowing where the developmental trajectory leads might prove highly valuable in understanding attachment processes in adolescence.

Bowlby (1973) referred to the attachment behavioral system as biologically prewired and evolutionarily chosen, based on ethological observations that reflected the universality of attachment behaviors in most mammals, and in particular in primates and the human species. Furthermore, his suggestion that the quite helpless offspring of primates cannot survive on their own without the protection of an older, wiser, and stronger ally was so compelling that the universality postulation was clearly invoked. Thus, the formation of the attachment bond was accepted as evolutionarily chosen and necessary for survival in infancy. However, the necessity of attachment relationships to survival in older children and still more in adulthood is not as clear. In fact, with age, the importance and centrality of attachment in one's life diminish, though this function remains to receive protection and get help with emotional and behavioral regulation during distress.

The literature on close relationships (Diamond & Hicks, 2004) documents that people in close relationships, particularly those who enjoy a unique close relationship, probably an attachment one, live longer and enjoy better well-being. Thus, the protective function of a close relationship, especially an attachment relationship, remains operative even in adolescence and adulthood. However, its essentiality for survival is much reduced compared with infancy and early childhood. Adolescents and adults are much better at protecting themselves and mobilizing other sources besides their attachment figures to receive protection. In fact, their survival is largely not dependent on their attachment figures, so we would argue that the natural selection processes that promoted the continuing operation of this behavioral system in adulthood are much elastic and less restrictive.

Accordingly it has been observed (Fraley et al., 2005) that whereas attachment processes in infancy and early childhood (before puberty) are fairly universal among primates and humans, the formation of a committed, moderately stable sexual pair-bond is not. Very few mammals and primates form such pair-bonds, and in fact the formation of committed, stable sexual pair-bonds is the exception, not the rule, in primates. Even in the human species, it is not clear whether committed pair-bonds are the rule. Examination of various cultures and subcultures in the present as well as throughout recorded history depicts a variable set of social bondings in which stable pair-bonds are but one arrangement. For example, ethnographic reports of contemporary hunter-gatherer tribes demonstrate that in such tribes, though pair-bonds are formed by most men and women, they are not universal. Pair-bonds do not seem to be stable, and pair-bonding may be mostly described as a serial monogamy. The stable constellation of bonding in the social group is with age-mates who grew up together (Caporael, 2001) or kin from the larger family, including parents and siblings. Other constellations in which attachment bonds seem to operate in adulthood may include a gender division in which men bond with other men, mostly kin, and women with other women, again mostly kin.

It has been suggested (Hazan, Gur-Yaish, & Campa, 2004) that the human species, unlike other primates, has evolved uniquely to develop attachment pair-bonds to promote paternal investment in the offspring, necessary because of the longer duration of the infant's dependency on the mother. However, recent evolutionary analyses (Fraley et al., 2005) have demonstrated that paternal involvement is much more prevalent, and probably started far earlier in evolutionary history than pair-bonding. If anything, paternal investment led in some cultures to pair-bonding rather than the reverse.

In line with these observations, examination of adults' networks of attachment relationships (Doherty & Feeney, 2004; Trinke & Bartholomew, 1997) revealed that these tend to include several figures (the mean seems to revolve around five) and that although romantic partners are central, there are other figures that are perceived as primary, such as parents, peers, or siblings. In particular, for most participants, parents were still part of the attachment network, often occupying a central position.

Together these different sources suggest that the transfer of attachment functions from parents to peers, and eventually the creation of an attachment romantic pair-bond, cannot be conceived as the ontological and developmental end point of the attachment system. Instead, the current observations seem to suggest that the main normative developmental trajectory involves two major processes: (1) attenuation in the importance of attachment relationships for the survival of the individual and (2) diversification of emotional investments. Adolescents partially transfer emotional investment from parents to peers and romantic partners, yet not to replace them fully as attachment figures but to diversify. This diversification, construed here as a developmental task, is manifested in the increase in number of attachment figures to whom one is attached, the lower levels of centrality accorded to each figure, and specialization of different figures in different situations or conditions (for example, turning to Mom when in physical pain and to best friend when emotionally hurt).

Convergence and Diversity in Working Models of Attachment

How do these processes affect adolescents' internal working models of attachment? Research on infancy and early childhood attachment patterns demonstrated that children form specific relationships with each attachment figure and that these relationships are quite independent in their quality. Some of these relationships may be more central than others in terms of their effects on child's outcomes, yet each may have distinct effects (Cassidy, 1999).

Interestingly, in late adolescence, the application of the Adult Attachment Interview resulted in the assignment of a classification into one overarching state of mind with respect to attachment, reflecting one central way in which this individual deals with attachment-related emotions, cognitions, and behaviors. Thus, children start by having several somewhat independent attachment models; by late adolescence, these seem to converge into a general model or state of mind with regard to attachment that guides relationships with new people as well as one's parenting (Allen & Land, 1999). This results in the attachment model becoming more a property of the individual: a personality attribute that individuals carry with them to other circumstances, other encounters, and other roles rather than a property of the specific relationships.

By contrast, several recent studies have demonstrated that in late adolescence, individuals still hold different and somewhat independent models of attachment. For example, in a study administering the AAI to adolescents separately with regard to mothers and fathers, Furman and Simon (2004) found that states of mind with regard to each figure, though quite highly correlated, were still distinct. Similar findings were reported in relationships with parents, friends, and romantic partners (Furman, Simon, Shaffer, & Bouchey, 2002). Although classifications based on interviews modeled after the AAI were generally alike, a moderate degree of dissimilarity existed among the models. This dissimilarity was mostly apparent when comparing internal models of attachment relationships with parents and romantic partners. Similarly, only a moderate level of similarity was reported in adulthood when relationships with parents and romantic partner in a committed relationship were assessed (Owens, Crowell, Pan, & Treboux, 1995).

These findings suggest that in late adolescence and young adulthood, individuals hold a general overarching model that reflects in general their personality in terms of regulating attachment-related emotions, cognitions and behaviors, and a large number of specific models. These specific models can reflect relationships with specific people, different levels of consciousness, and also different roles—offspring, friend, romantic partner. (For a full discussion, see Bretherton & Munholland, 1999; Chen, Boucher, & Tapias, 2006.)

Thus, two developmental processes occur in the period from infancy to adolescence: convergence of attachment models, on the one hand, and an increase in diversity, variety, and heterogeneity, on the other. How do these two processes co-occur? We believe that the process of convergence and the emergence of a general dominant way of addressing attachment issues are still apparent prior to adolescence, probably already in early childhood. The seeming emergence of consolidation in adolescence may be a result of the tool used to assess individual differences at this age, the AAI. In fact, assessment of attachment models with fathers and mothers in middle childhood already shows moderately high convergence (Kerns, Tomich, & Kim, 2006). We suggest that although further convergence of models occurs in adolescence, the major developmental process of adolescence with regard to internal models is a leap in complexity, flexibility, and sophistication.

First, the adolescent's cognitive and emotional capacity to reflect on the various relationships, augmented by emotional distancing from parents, fosters a process of change and flexibility as opposed to automatic activation of various cognitive, emotional, and behavioral tendencies. Second, diversification in attachment relationships, and the addition of different figures with whom attachment functions are experienced, opens the way for a diversity in the adolescent's attachment models and possible change in the dominant model if the adolescent has one. Experimentation with various relationships extends the repertoire of perceptions, emotions, and behaviors regarding attachment and promotes flexibility of working models. Finally, the capacity of adolescents more freely to choose with whom they want to form a relationship facilitates a process of compensation and a change in earlier models.

These developmental processes result in an intricate network of models that exist at varying levels of specificity and awareness and allow high flexibility in activation, as well as open the way to changes in dominant models.

Individual Differences

State of mind with regard to attachment reflects differences in capacity for flexibility of attentional processes pertaining to attachment (Main, 1991; Maier et al., 2004). Previous conceptualizations also suggested that it entails generalized expectations regarding the self and close relationships and various emotion-regulation and social competencies (Kobak, Cole, Ferenz-Gillies, Fleming, & Gamble, 1993). As such, it is implicated in affecting the way adolescents meet the developmental tasks of adolescence.

In general, an autonomous state of mind equips adolescents with the optimal resources, competencies, and familial contexts for coping with the developmental tasks of adolescence. Autonomous adolescents should cope more easily with the ontogenetic tasks of distancing from parents, demonstrating autonomous self-reliance, forging close relations with peers and romantic partners, and diversifying emotional investments. Attachment security has been associated with the capacity to balance autonomy and relatedness in the relationship with parents (Allen, Hauser, Bell, & O'Connor, 1994; Allen et al., 2003; Kobak et al., 1993). Furthermore, adolescent attachment security was positively associated with adolescent deidealization of mother and with maternal attunement and support (Allen et al., 2003). It might be easier and safer to argue with your parents when their consistent secure base is guaranteed.

Security of attachment was also associated with positive qualities of friendships such as closeness, an elaborate concept of friendship, and good emotional regulation abilities in times of conflict with best friends (Zimmermann, 2004), as well as with having secure working models of relationships with friends (Furman et al., 2002). Moreover it was associated with integration in the peer group and social acceptance (Allen, Moore, Kuperminc, & Bell, 1998; Zimmermann, 2004), positive dyadic interactions with the romantic partner (Roisman, Madsen, Hennighausen, Sroufe, & Collins, 2001), and higher capacity for mature intimacy in friendships and romantic relationships (Scharf et al., 2004). Among at-risk sixteen year olds, security was related to having first intercourse at a later age (O'Beirne & Allen, 1996) and with having fewer sexual partners and greater use of contraception (Moore, 1997). This might imply a "quality-versus-quantity" approach to sexual relationships (Allen & Land, 1999, p. 327; Belsky, 1999).

With regard to the capacity for autonomous and self-reliant functioning, autonomous individuals were rated by others (observers or peers) as more ego resilient, less anxious, and less hostile than insecure individuals, and security was associated with increases in social skills from ages sixteen to eighteen (Allen et al., 2002; Kobak & Sceery, 1988; Zimmermann, 1999).

Coping with the demands of military basic training (the normative home-leaving experience for compulsory military service for Israeli men at age eighteen), autonomous individuals reported using more problem-focused coping than did dismissing individuals, and their peers in basic training perceived them to cope instrumentally and socially better than their dismissing counterparts. During this stressful transition, they also perceived their parents as more sensitively responsive to them than did dismissing individuals (Scharf et al., 2004). In a different context Larose, Bernier, and Tarabulsy (2005) found that autonomous individuals showed better learning dispositions throughout the college transition. Seiffge-Krenke and Beyers (2005) found that secure individuals became more competent in dealing with different stressors from early adolescence to young adulthood. In sum, compared with others, autonomous adolescents probably find the developmental path of adolescence smoother and more gradual, and they cope better with its tasks.

Coping with the challenges of the developmental tasks of adolescence is less optimal for insecure adolescents. The trajectories might be different for preoccupied and dismissing individuals. Generally the evidence so far suggests that preoccupied individuals find the developmental tasks of adolescence more challenging than dismissing individuals do.

Preoccupation was associated with depression (Kobak et al., 1991; Allen et al., 1998) and thoughts of suicide (Adam, Sheldon, Adrienne, & West, 1996), more interpersonal difficulties, and more symptoms than in others (Brown & Wright, 2003). Preoccupation was further linked to an increase in delinquency from ages sixteen to eighteen (Allen et al., 2002). Preoccupied students who left home and moved to college experienced more stress over their family and reported more negative relationships with both parents, yet they had more contact with parents than autonomous individuals did (Bernier, Larose, & Whipple, 2005). Throughout the college transition, preoccupied individuals reported more fear of failure during the first semester, felt less comfortable seeking help from their teachers, and gave lower priority to their studies (Larose et al., 2005). Finally, compared with others, preoccupied individuals were viewed as less ego resilient and more anxious by peers and reported high levels of personal distress, while viewing their family as more supportive than the dismissing group did (Kobak & Sceery, 1988).

The lower functioning of preoccupied girls compared with others, especially across the transition away from home to compulsory military service, was underscored in another study (Scharf & Mayseless, 2005). Preoccupied girls evinced the worst adjustment and coping, as reported by them, their mothers, and their peers. They reported the highest levels of distress and lowest levels of well-being, emotional adjustment, and commitment to the service. Their mothers viewed them as sad, stressed, and malfunctioning and with the highest level of social problems. Their peers similarly viewed them as the saddest.

The findings on dismissing individuals are less clear. In general, dismissing adolescents were more likely to evince substance abuse and conduct disorders (Brown & Wright, 2003) and were less likely to adjust well to the transition away from home. For example, dismissing individuals reported less preparation for examinations and diminished attention throughout the transition to college (Larose et al., 2005), were rated higher on hostility by peers, and reported more distant relationships in terms of more loneliness and low levels of social support from family (Kobak & Sceery, 1988). They (only boys) further evinced lower levels of intimacy in relations with friends and romantic partners and lower levels of coping with compulsory military service (Scharf et al., 2004).

However, in several studies, dismissing individuals proved quite similar to autonomous ones in their functioning. For example, dismissing girls were not different from autonomous girls in their coping and adjustment to compulsory military service in their self-reports and in the reports by mothers and friends (Scharf & Mayseless, 2005). And dismissing boys were similar to autonomous ones on indicators of individuation (Scharf et al., 2004). Some of the developmental tasks of adolescence, in particular distancing from parents, developing autonomous self-reliance, and diversifying emotional investments, perhaps do not pose such a difficult challenge to dismissing adolescents as they do to preoccupied ones. By contrast, forging intimate relations that evince attachment functions with peers may be a more challenging task for dismissing than for preoccupied individuals (Scharf et al., 2004).

Most of the studies described here did not examine ontogenetic developmental processes even when they employed a longitudinal design. For example, data on how adolescents with different states of mind cope with the developmental expectation to decrease emotional investment in parents, or evidence whether or how internal models of different kinds become more flexible and sophisticated, is scarce. In the context of individual differences in attachment, there is also very little indication regarding the longitudinal process of diversification and the question of whether close relationships with peers or investment in self-reliance serve as compensation for decreased investment in parents.

As a preliminary examination of this direction, Freeman and Brown (2001) found that secure adolescents (identified using a projective measure) favored mothers over best friends, romantic partners, and fathers as attachment figures, whereas insecure adolescents indicated a strong preference for boyfriend or girlfriend as their primary target for attachment, and nearly a third of dismissing individuals identified themselves as their primary attachment figure. These interesting findings, as well as other questions related to the way adolescents with different attachment models traverse the developmental tasks of adolescence, await examination in future research.

Discussion

Four developmental tasks of adolescence were described here as involved in the ontogenetic developmental processes that characterize attachment in adolescence: weakening of emotional investment in relationships with parents, developing autonomous self reliance—individuation, forging close relations with peers and romantic partners in which reciprocity is apparent, and diversifying emotional investments. Some of these tasks, in particular the achievement of autonomy and independence from parents and the formation of close relationships with peers, are central tasks in most conceptualizations regarding developmental tasks in adolescence (Schoeppe & Havighurst, 1952). One of the contributions of this chapter is embedding them as part of an expected ontogenetic developmental process of the behavioral system of attachment, thus suggesting a conceptual integration of psychoanalytical thinking with the general literature on developmental processes in adolescence and attachment.

This transitional period might be hazardous for adolescents. The figures to whom attachment needs are directed are often less stable and are less committed to the adolescents in the long run. They are not equipped with evolutionary tendencies to protect the adolescent, and they themselves (in case of peers) may be simultaneously in need. Turning away from parents in the service of promoting adolescents' individuation, self-reliance, maturity, and finding a sex mate outside one's gene pool may leave adolescents more vulnerable and may lead to increased feelings of anxiety and loneliness (Blos, 1967; Youniss & Smollar, 1989).

Together, these changes expose and instigate vulnerabilities, as well as open up possibilities of change and flexibility in individuals' attachment models as the network of attachment strategies or models becomes more complex and elaborate. These developmental tasks are postulated to occur in order to allow diversion of sexual drives away from parents and outside the individual's gene pool to nonkin and to promote the higher self-reliance and flexibility needed for survival in adulthood.

The research literature on adolescence provides some empirical support for these postulations; however, much is still open. Let us illuminate several such future research avenues. First, there is a need for longitudinal studies that document and highlight the developmental processes described here. Attachment researchers have often examined continuity of individual differences, but for most cases, they have not investigated general universal developmental processes. For example, does increased emotional investment in peers come as compensation for decreased investment in parents? How do distancing from parents and investment in peers relate to investment in self to enhance self-reliance and autonomy? Do identification with idols and membership in actual and symbolic groups serve the same functions of emotional investment? Are all these channels of investment complementary?

It is important to note that in most previous studies, researchers who examined several relationships concurrently investigated the quality of the different relationships and examined similarity among them; here we suggest examining the level of emotional investment in each relationship. This is similar to the idea of cathexis and the notion discussed by Ainsworth (1989) and then by Berlin and Cassidy (1999), regarding the extent that a relationship "penetrates one's different aspects of life" (Ainsworth, 1989, p. 36). Researchers might need to find ways to assess this aspect. One possibility is to employ or develop sophisticated tools, such as the ones used by cognitive and social psychologists that include priming and reaction times.

Another research question is related to the place of puberty. Are these developmental processes related to puberty, and if so, in what ways? Are they related to the onset of puberty? Or might we be able to observe a continual synchrony between the physical and hormonal changes and these social and emotional changes by employing dynamic systems' approaches?

Thus far we know very little about these longitudinal processes of change in the context of individual differences in models of attachment. This is clearly different from concurrent, cross-sectional comparisons of individuals with different attachment patterns. For example, do secure individuals also distance from their parents? How can we assess their expected continual trust and closeness with their parents while also examining such distancing? What characterizes dismissing and preoccupied adolescents in this regard?

Another issue to address is gender differences. In general, researchers have claimed that girls mature and define their identity through connectedness, whereas boys mature and define their identity through separation and autonomy (Josselson, 1996). Historically, attachment quality and attachment processes were seen as similar for the two genders. However, there are some indications that by middle childhood, various gender differences have emerged (Kerns, Schlegelmilch, Morgan, & Abraham, 2005). Such differences in the normative trajectory of development might be even more pronounced in adolescence and need to be addressed in future research. For example, if adolescent girls tend to define their identity and individuation through connectedness, they might evince less of a need to distance from, and decrease emotional investment in, parents, and they may find it more difficult than boys to address this challenge.

In this chapter, we borrowed freely from the psychoanalytical literature and its insights, disregarding to some extent the important differences between these notions and attachment theory. For example, earlier psychoanalytical writers focused on internalized fantasy objects and stressed the need of adolescents to completely disengage from them and fight what they saw as infantile dependencies. This is clearly not our view here. We do not contend that relinquishing parents as attachment figures is desirable or normative. Still, it seems that in the efforts of attachment theory to counter psychoanalytical notions, attachment theory has played down the importance of the normative (evolutionary-based) processes of diminished emotional and behavioral investment in primary caregivers and the diversification of investment. The current approach that involves an attempt to apply insights from psychoanalytical conceptualizations to attachment processes accords with recent calls and attempts (Steele & Steele, 1998; Mayseless, 2005) to advance a cautious and thoughtful consideration of the merits and insights gained by the two paradigms—attachment and psychoanalysis—to developmental and clinical processes. Future research may need to address some of the speculative and challenging postulations discussed in this chapter.

The next five chapters in this volume similarly address central issues of attachment in adolescence. In Chapter Two, Allen and Manning address the changing nature and function of the attachment system and contend that in adolescence, the frequency of true survival threats diminishes greatly, but the importance of regulating affect through social interactions is maintained. In line with this observation, they suggest that it is possible to view attachment behavior as distinct from but also as a precursor to broader patterns of social affect regulation.

Dykas and Cassidy focus in Chapter Three on processes of social information that characterize various internal working models. They review the links between attachment and attachment-relevant social information processing and discuss how it is expressed during adolescence in memory, feedback seeking, perceptions of others, and secure base scripts.

In Chapter Four, Kobak, Rosenthal, Zajac, and Madsen discuss the formation of hierarchies of attachment relationships in adolescence in which peers play an important role. The authors underscore the importance of addressing who is identified as an attachment figure, how these bonds are organized in hierarchies of relationships, and how and when peer relationships are transformed to attachment bonds, and they suggest various future directions for research.

Kiang and Furman discuss in Chapter Five the issue of concordance of representations of attachment to parents in adolescent siblings raised in the same family. They argue that a simple conceptual model leading us to expect concordant adolescent siblings' representations is not confirmed. They thus suggest explanations for the modest degree of childhood and adolescent siblings' similarity and its implications for attachment theory.

Finally, in Chapter Six, Carlivati and Collins focus on issues of continuity and change in attachment representations in adolescence in a sample at risk because of early poverty. They highlight the empirical evidence regarding attachment stability and change in a risk sample and discuss the reasons that adolescence may be a period of attachment security change in this population.

References

Adam, K. S., Sheldon, K., Adrienne, E., & West, M. (1996). Attachment organization and history of suicidal behavior in clinical adolescents. *Journal of Consulting and Clinical Psychology, 64*, 264–272.
Ainsworth, M. S. (1989). Attachments beyond infancy. *American Psychologist, 44*, 709–716.

Allen, J. P., Hauser, S. T., Bell, K. L., & O'Connor, T. G. (1994). Longitudinal assessment of autonomy and relatedness in adolescent-family interactions as predictors of adolescent ego development and self-esteem. *Child Development, 65,* 179–194.

Allen, J. P., & Land, D. (1999). Attachment in adolescence. In J. Cassidy & P. R. Shaver (Eds.), *Handbook of attachment: Theory, research, and clinical applications* (pp. 319–335). New York: Guilford Press.

Allen, J. P., McElhaney, K. B., Land, D. J., Kuperminc, G. P., Moore, C. W., O'Beirne-Kelly, H., & Kilmer, S. L (2003). A secure base in adolescence: Markers of attachment security in the mother-adolescent relationship. *Child Development, 74,* 292–307.

Allen, J. P., Moore, C., Kuperminc, G., & Bell, K. (1998). Attachment and adolescent psychosocial functioning. *Child Development, 69,* 1406–1419.

Ammaniti, M., van IJzendoorn, M. H., Speranza, A. M., & Tambelli, R. (2000). Internal working models of attachment during late childhood and early adolescence: An exploration of stability and change. *Attachment and Human Development, 2,* 328–346.

Belsky, J. (1999). Interactional and contextual determinants of attachment security. In J. Cassidy & P. R. Shaver (Eds.), *Handbook of attachment: Theory, research, and clinical applications* (pp. 249–264). New York: Guilford Press.

Berlin, L. J., & Cassidy, J. (1999). Relations among relationships: Contributions from attachment theory and research. In J. Cassidy & P. R. Shaver (Eds.), *Handbook of attachment: Theory, research, and clinical applications* (pp. 688–712). New York: Guilford Press.

Bernier, A., Larose, S., & Whipple, N. (2005). Leaving home for college: A potentially stressful event for adolescents with preoccupied attachment patterns. *Attachment and Human Development, 7,* 171–185.

Blos, P. (1962). *On adolescence: A psychoanalytic interpretation.* New York: Free Press.

Blos, P. (1967). *The adolescent passage.* New York: International Universities Press.

Bowlby, J. (1973). *Attachment and loss: Vol. 2. Separation and anxiety.* New York: Basic Books.

Bretherton, I., & Munholland, K. A. (1999). Internal working models in attachment relationships: A construct revisited. In J. Cassidy & P. R. Shaver (Eds.), *Handbook of attachment: Theory, research and clinical applications* (pp. 89–111). New York: Guilford Press.

Brown, B. B. (2004). Adolescents' relationships with peers. In R. M. Lerner & L. Steinberg (Eds.), *Handbook of adolescent psychology* (pp. 363–394). Hoboken, NJ: Wiley.

Brown, B. B., & Klute, C. (2003). Friendships, cliques, and crowds. In G. R. Adams & M. D. Berzonsky (Eds.), *Blackwell handbook of adolescence* (pp. 330–348). Oxford: Blackwell.

Brown, L. S., & Wright, J. (2003). The relationship between attachment strategies and psychopathology in adolescence. *Psychology and Psychotherapy: Theory, Research and Practice, 76,* 351–367.

Caporael, L. R. (2001). Parts and wholes: The evolutionary importance of groups. In C. Sedikides & M. B. Brewer (Eds.), *Individual self, relational self, collective self* (pp. 241–258). Philadelphia: Psychology Press.

Carver, K., Joyner, K., & Udry, J. R. (2003). In P. Florsheim (Ed.), *Adolescent romantic relations and sexual behavior: Theory, research, and practical implications* (pp. 23–56). Mahwah, NJ: Erlbaum.

Cassidy, J. (1999). The nature of the child's ties. In J. Cassidy & P. R. Shaver (Eds.), *Handbook of attachment: Theory, research, and clinical applications* (pp. 3–20). New York: Guilford Press.

Chen, S., Boucher, H. C., & Tapias, M. P. (2006). The relational self revealed: Integrative conceptualization and implications for interpersonal life. *Psychological Bulletin, 132,* 151–179.

Collins, W. A., & Laursen, B. (2004). Parent-adolescent relationships and influences. In R. Lerner & L. Steinberg (Eds.), *Handbook of adolescent psychology* (2nd ed., pp. 331–361). Hoboken, NJ: Wiley.

Collins, W. A., & Steinberg, L. (2006). Adolescent development in interpersonal context. In N. Eisenberg, W. Damon, & R. Lerner (Eds.), *Handbook of child psychology: Vol. 3. Social, emotional, and personality development* (pp. 1003–1067). Hoboken, NJ: Wiley.

Conger, R. D., & Ge, X. (1999). Conflict and cohesion in parent-adolescent relations: Changes in emotional expression from early to midadolescence. In M. J. Cox & J. Brooks-Gunn (Eds.), *Conflict and cohesion in families: Causes and consequences* (pp. 185–206). Mahwah, NJ: Erlbaum.

Diamond, L. M., & Hicks, A. M. (2004). Psychobiological perspectives on attachment: Implications for health over the lifespan. In W. S. Rholes, & J. A. Simpson (Eds.), *Adult attachment: Theory, research, and clinical implications* (pp. 240–263). New York: Guilford Press.

Doherty, N. A., & Feeney, J. A. (2004). The composition of attachment networks throughout the adult years. *Personal Relationships, 11,* 469–488.

Ford, C. S., & Beach, F. A. (1951). *Patterns of sexual behavior.* New York: HarperCollins.

Fraley, R. C., Brumbaugh, C. C., & Marks, M. J. (2005). The evolution and function of adult attachment: A comparative and phylogenetic analysis. *Journal of Personality and Social Psychology, 89,* 731–746.

Freeman, H., & Brown, B. B. (2001). Primary attachment to parents and peers during adolescence: Differences by attachment style. *Journal of Youth and Adolescence, 30,* 653–674.

Freud, A. (1958). Adolescence. *Psychoanalytic Study of the Child, 13,* 255–278.

Furman, W., & Buhrmester, D. (1992). Age and sex differences in perceptions of networks of personal relationships. *Child Development, 63,* 103–115.

Furman, W., & Simon, V. A. (2004). Concordance in attachment states of mind and styles with respect to fathers and mothers. *Developmental Psychology, 40,* 1239–1247.

Furman, W., Simon, V. A., Shaffer, L., & Bouchey, H. A. (2002). Adolescents' working models and styles for relationships with parents, friends, and romantic partners. *Child Development, 73,* 241–255.

Furman, W., & Wehner, E. A. (1997). Adolescent romantic relationships: A developmental perspective. In S. Shulman & W. A. Collins (Eds.), *Romantic relationships in adolescence: Developmental perspectives* (pp. 21–36). San Francisco: Jossey-Bass.

Giles, D. C., & Maltby, J. (2004). The role of media figures in adolescent development: Relations between autonomy, attachment, and interest in celebrities. *Personality and Individual Differences, 36,* 813–822.

Hardy, C. L., Bukowski, W. M., & Sippola, L. K. (2002). Stability and change in peer relationships during the transition to middle-level school. *Journal of Early Adolescence, 22,* 117–142.

Hazan, C., Gur-Yaish, N., & Campa, M. (2004). What does it mean to be attached? In W. S. Rholes & J. A. Simpson (Eds.), *Adult attachment: Theory, research, and clinical implications* (pp. 55–85). New York: Guilford Press.

Hazan, C., Hutt, M., Sturgeon, J., & Bricker, T. (1991, April). *The process of relinquishing parents as attachment figures.* Paper presented at the biennial meeting of the Society for Research in Child Development, Seattle, WA.

Hazan, C., & Zeifman, D. (1994). Sex and the psychological tether. In K. Bartholomew & D. Perlman (Eds.), *Advances in personal relationships: Vol. 5. Attachment processes in adulthood* (pp. 151–178). London: Jessica Kingsley.

Josselson, R. (1980). Ego development in adolescence. In J. Adelson (Ed.), *Handbook of adolescent psychology* (pp. 188–210). Hoboken, NJ: Wiley.

Josselson, R. (1996). *Revisiting herself: The story of women's identity from college to midlife.* New York: Oxford University Press.

Kerns, K. A., Tomich, P. L., & Kim, P. (2006). Normative trends in children's perceptions of availability and utilization of attachment figures in middle childhood. *Social Development, 15,* 1-22.

Kerns, K. A., Schlegelmilch, A., Morgan, T. A., & Abraham, M. M. (2005). Assessing attachment in middle childhood. In K. A. Kerns & R. Richardson (Eds.), *Attachment in middle childhood* (pp. 46–70). New York: Guilford Press.

Kobak, R. R., Cole, H. E., Ferenz-Gillies, R., Fleming, W. S., & Gamble, W. (1993). Adult Attachment Interview and emotion regulation during mother-teen problem solving: A control theory analysis. *Child Development, 64,* 231–245.

Kobak, R. R., & Sceery, A. (1988). Attachment in late adolescence: Working models, affect regulation and representations of self and others. *Child Development, 59,* 135–146.

Lapsley, D. K. (1993). Toward an integrated theory of adolescent ego development: The "new look" at adolescent egocentrism. *American Journal of Orthopsychiatry, 63,* 562–571.

Larose, S., & Bernier, A. (2001). Social support processes: Mediators of attachment state of mind and adjustment in late adolescence. *Attachment and Human Development, 3,* 96–120.

Larose, S., Bernier, A., & Tarabulsy, G. M. (2005). Attachment state of mind, learning dispositions, and academic performance during the college transition. *Developmental Psychology, 41,* 281–289.

Larson, R. W., Richards, M. H., Moneta, G., Holmbeck, G., & Duckett, E. (1996). Changes in adolescents' daily interactions with their families from 10 to 18: Disengagement and transformation. *Developmental Psychology, 32,* 744–754.

Maier, M. A., Bernier, A., Perkrun, R., Zimmermann, P., & Grossmann, K. E. (2004). Attachment working models as unconscious structures: An experimental test. *International Journal of Behavioral Development, 28,* 180–189.

Main, M. (1991). Metacognitive knowledge, metacognitive monitoring, and singular (coherent) vs. multiple (incoherent) model of attachment: Findings and directions for future research. In C. M. Parkes, H. J. Stevenson, & P. Marris (Eds.), *Attachment across the life cycle* (pp. 127–159). New York: Tavistock/Routledge.

Mayseless, O. (2005). Ontogeny of attachment in middle childhood: Conceptualization of normative changes. In K. A. Kerns & R. A. Richardson (Eds.), *Attachment in middle childhood* (pp. 1–23). New York: Guilford Press.

Moore, C. W. (1997). *Models of attachment, relationships with parents, and sexual behavior in at-risk adolescents.* Unpublished doctoral dissertation, University of Virginia.

O'Beirne, H. A., & Allen. J. P. (1996, March). *Adolescent sexual behavior: Individual, peer and family correlates.* Paper presented at the biennial meeting of the Society for Research on Adolescence, Boston.

Owens, G., Crowell, J., Pan, H., & Treboux, D. (1995). The prototype hypothesis and the origins of attachment working models: Adult relationships with parents and romantic partners. *Monographs of the Society for Research in Child Development, 60,* 216–233.

Roisman, G. I., Madsen, S. D., Hennighausen, K. H., & Sroufe, L. A., & Collins, W. A. (2001). The coherence of dyadic behavior across parent-child and romantic relationships as mediated by the internalized representation of experience. *Attachment and Human Development, 3,* 156–172.

Rycroft, C. (1995). *A critical dictionary of psychoanalysis* (2nd ed.). New York: Penguin Press.

Salt, R. E. (1991). Affectionate touch between fathers and preadolescent sons. *Journal of Marriage and the Family, 53,* 545–554.

Scharf, M. (2001). A "natural experiment" in childrearing ecologies and adolescents' attachment and separation representations. *Child Development, 72,* 236–251.

Scharf, M., & Mayseless, O. (2001). The capacity for romantic intimacy: Exploring the contribution of best friend and marital and parental relationships. *Journal of Adolescence, 24,* 379–399.

Scharf, M., & Mayseless, O. (2004, July). *Relationships between parents and their emerging adults' children: Do these hearts grow fonder?* Paper presented at the Biennial Meeting of the International Society for the Study of Behavioral Development, Ghent, Belgium.

Scharf, M., & Mayseless, O. (2005, April). *Away from home: Adolescents' attachment representations and adaptation to the leaving-home transition.* Paper presented at the biennial meeting of Society for Research in Child Development, Atlanta, GA.

Scharf, M., & Mayseless, O., & Kivenson-Baron, I. (2004). Adolescents' attachment representations and developmental tasks in emerging adulthood. *Developmental Psychology, 40,* 430–444.

Schoeppe, A., & Havighurst, R. J. (1952). A validation of development and adjustment hypotheses of adolescence. *Journal of Educational Psychology, 43,* 339–353.

Scholte, R.H.J., van Lieshout, C.F.M., & van Aken, M.A.G. (2001). Perceived relational support in adolescence: Dimensions, configurations, and adolescent adjustment. *Journal of Research on Adolescence, 11,* 71–94.

Schulenberg, J. E., Bryant, A. L., & O'Malley, P. M. (2004). Taking hold of some kind of life: How developmental tasks relate to trajectories of well-being during the transition to adulthood. *Development and Psychopathology, 16,* 1119–1140.

Seiffge-Krenke, I., & Beyers, W. (2005). Coping trajectories from adolescence to young adulthood: Links to attachment state of mind. *Journal of Research on Adolescence, 15,* 561–582.

Shulman, S., & Scharf, M. (2000). Adolescent romantic behaviors and perceptions: Age- and gender-related differences, and links with family and peer relationships. *Journal of Research on Adolescence, 10,* 99–118.

Steele, H., & Steele, M. (1998). Attachment and psychoanalysis: Time for a reunion. *Social Development, 7,* 92-119.

Steinberg, L. (1987). Bound to bicker. *Psychology Today, 21,* 36–39.

Steinberg, L. (1990). Autonomy, conflict, and harmony in the family relationship. In S. S. Feldman & G. R. Elliott (Eds.), *At the threshold: The developing adolescent* (pp. 255–276). Cambridge, MA: Harvard University Press.

Steinberg, L., & Silk, J. S. (2002). Parenting adolescents. In M. H. Bornstein (Ed.), *Handbook of parenting: Vol. 1. Children and parenting* (2nd ed., pp. 103–133). Mahwah, NJ: Erlbaum.

Stierlin, H. (1981). *Separating parents and adolescents: Individuation in the family.* New York: Jason Aronson.

Trinke, S. J., & Bartholomew, K. (1997). Hierarchies of attachment relationships in young adulthood. *Journal of Social and Personal Relationships, 14,* 603–625.

Youniss, J., & Smollar, J. (1989). Adolescents' interpersonal relationships in social context. In T. J. Berndt & G. W. Ladd (Eds.), *Peer relationships in child development* (pp. 300–316). Hoboken, NJ: Wiley.

Zani, B. (1993). Dating and interpersonal relationships in adolescence. In S. Jackson & T. H. Rodriguez (Eds.), *Adolescence and its social worlds* (pp. 95–119). Mahwah, NJ: Erlbaum.

Zarit, S. H., & Eggebeen, D. J. (2002). Parent-child relationships in adulthood and later years. In M. H. Bornstein (Ed.), *Handbook of parenting: Vol. 1. Children and parenting* (2nd ed., pp. 135–161). Mahwah, NJ: Erlbaum.

Zimmermann, P. (1999). Structure and functions of internal working models of attachment and their role for emotion regulation. *Attachment and Human Development, 1,* 291–306.

Zimmermann, P. (2004). Attachment representations and characteristics of friendship relations during adolescence. *Journal of Experimental Child Psychology, 88,* 83–101.

MIRI SCHARF *is a professor of developmental psychology in the Faculty of Education, University of Haifa, Israel, and the head of the educational counseling program.*

OFRA MAYSELESS *is a professor of developmental psychology and the dean of the faculty of education at the University of Haifa in Israel.*

2

This chapter addresses the changing nature and function of the attachment system as it develops into adolescence and becomes intertwined with broader patterns of affect regulation.

From Safety to Affect Regulation: Attachment from the Vantage Point of Adolescence

Joseph P. Allen, Nell Manning

> The extraordinary intricacy of all the factors to be taken into consideration leaves only one way of presenting them open to us. We must select first one and then another point of view, and follow it up through the material as long as the application of it seems to yield results.
>
> Sigmund Freud (1915)

John Bowlby (1969/1982) opens the first book of his classic *Attachment* trilogy with this quotation from Sigmund Freud in a chapter titled "Point of View." Bowlby then goes on to carefully outline his own paradigm-altering point of view, building from extensive observations of young children separated from their parents. Bowlby's selection of this quotation suggests his recognition that viewing attachment from the perspective of the young child, although remarkably productive and generative, should ultimately be just one of a number of vantage points from which we view attachment phenomena. This chapter suggests one such additional point of view.

We begin with a thought experiment. What if the Adult Attachment Interview (AAI; George, Kaplan, & Main, 1996; Main, Goldwyn, & Hesse,

---

This chapter was completed with the assistance of grants from the National Institute of Mental Health.

NEW DIRECTIONS FOR CHILD AND ADOLESCENT DEVELOPMENT, no. 117, Fall 2007 © Wiley Periodicals, Inc.
Published online in Wiley InterScience (www.interscience.wiley.com) • DOI: 10.1002/cd.192

2002) had come first? What if we started not with the study of infants but of adolescents? And what if the AAI originated not from attachment theory and data from the Strange Situation (a measure designed to assess the quality of the infant's attachment to his or her caregiver), but from other perspectives on human behavior? Looking afresh at the AAI and its classification system from this vantage point, we might first simply observe that we had a measure that asked adolescents and adults about childhood relationships and then coded the degree of coherence with which the resulting emotion-laden memories emerged.

Although childhood relationships are clearly the focus of the interview, the primary emphasis in coding the interviews would not be on the quality of those relationships—even people with horrific childhood relationships can be rated high in "autonomy" and "coherence"—but on how those relationships were discussed. Nor would the AAI, at least on its face, appear to be primarily assessing a "safety regulating system" as Bowlby (1969/1982) describes infant attachment. Rather, what we might notice is that some individuals in the AAI appear to shy away from discussing strong emotional experiences from childhood. Others appear to get easily lost in such discussions. And still others are able to coherently balance recountings of intensive emotional experiences with thoughtful evaluations of those experiences.

Interestingly, even without any attachment context, the AAI remains a useful and intriguing measure. We might readily conclude that it captures an adolescent's or adult's ability to manage strong affect in recounting emotionally charged memories. Most (although not all) of these memories are solicited around childhood experiences with attachment figures, but whether this focus is critical would not at first glance be apparent. If the infant Strange Situation were subsequently developed and linked to parental AAI classifications, we might use this as further evidence that the AAI was capturing an aspect of affect regulation that was fundamental not so much to a parent's attachment behavior as to his or her capacity for sensitive caregiving behavior.

The point here is not that we could envision a world in which infant attachment behavior takes on a secondary role heuristically in explaining the meaning of the AAI. Rather, it is that considering attachment-related phenomena from the perspective of adolescence suggests new ways of thinking about attachment that may be enormously generative. In the remainder of this chapter, we seek not so much to reconsider the meaning of the AAI as to use this new point of view to examine the challenges that adolescent development presents for a broader attachment theory. Ultimately we would like to show that what we are proposing is far more than a thought experiment. As we move from infancy toward adulthood, attachment processes evolve and change qualitatively and fundamentally in nature. Recognizing these changes is likely to be central to continuing to advance our understanding of attachment as a life span phenomenon.

NEW DIRECTIONS FOR CHILD AND ADOLESCENT DEVELOPMENT • DOI: 10.1002/cd

Shifts in Perspective

Given that the vast majority of our research on attachment processes in adolescence has been done with the Adult Attachment Interview (George et al., 1996) or a version slightly adapted for adolescents (Ward & Carlson, 1995), it is important to be precise about the relation of this instrument to the construct it assesses. Given the remarkable power of the AAI in predicting infant offspring Strange Situation behavior (Main, Kaplan, & Cassidy, 1985), it is tempting to equate measure and construct and conclude that the AAI provides a direct window into precisely the same attachment system observed in infancy. Yet an indicator of a construct, even one with near perfect predictive power, is not the same as the construct. From both her explicit statements to her choice of labels for AAI classifications, Mary Main has made clear that it is premature to conclude that the AAI is simply the adult version of the infant Strange Situation (Main, 1999; Main & George, 1985). Recent research in adolescence bears out this cautionary note and forces several related shifts in perspective as we move from considering infant attachment behavior to adolescent attachment states of mind regarding attachment.

PERSPECTIVE SHIFT 1. *Adolescent attachment states of mind are not a direct reflection of infant attachment experiences and working models.*

Our first hint that adolescent AAIs have taken us beyond the world of infant attachment behavior comes as we examine the literature on long-term continuities in attachment behavior from infancy. Rather than robust relationships, we find somewhat tenuous links. Some studies find sizable correlations between infant attachment and future adolescent AAI security (Hamilton, 2000; Waters, Merrick, Treboux, Crowell, & Albersheim, 2000). Others find no such relationship but identify experiences beyond infancy that can account for some (though far from all) of the observed discontinuity (Weinfield, Sroufe, & Egeland, 2000). These studies span long periods of time with many important intervening variables. Instability is also found within infancy and within the same assessment technique. Thus, these findings provide only the first hint that, beginning in adolescence, links of attachment states of mind to actual attachment behavior may be less direct than expected. Security in adolescent states of mind is thus clearly not a direct translation of prior infant attachment relationships. It does not directly mirror the past, but what about the present?

PERSPECTIVE SHIFT 2. *Adolescent attachment states of mind are not a direct reflection of parental attachment status or of the current parent-adolescent relationship.*

If the AAI is not directly capturing qualities of prior infant-parent attachment relationships, what about the current family relationships of the adolescents who participate in this interview? Shouldn't adolescent states of mind closely and uniquely reflect either the attachment states of mind of their parents (as the Strange Situation does so remarkably well for infants) or the quality of the current adolescent-parent attachment relationship? In addressing this question, we begin first with our own disappointment. We have been collecting and coding adolescent AAIs in our lab for the past fifteen years on a variety of samples. In some of these, we have also obtained AAIs from the parents of our teenagers. Our first question was: Would we find the same degree of correspondence between teen and parent AAIs as others have found between parent AAIs and infant Strange Situation assessments? Alas, the answer has been negative. Yes, we find correspondence— but it is on the order of a .2 correlation between mother and teen security scores using Kobak's Q-Sort (Allen et al., 2003; Kobak, 1990). Others find similarly modest correspondences using the AAI classification system (Benoit & Parker, 1994).

What about actual parent-teen relationship behavior? Here we fare somewhat better. Indeed, we find that a combination of adolescent displays of autonomy and parental displays of sensitivity observed across a variety of contexts predicts as much as 40 percent of the variance in security in adolescent attachment states of mind (Allen et al., 2003). We have interpreted this pattern of behaviors as the adolescent analogue of the infant's exploration from a secure base. The infant explores the environment with physical distance from the parent. By adolescence, this exploration has become of cognitive and emotional distance from parents. So reviewing these data, we might conclude that the AAI really was capturing something unique to the parent-adolescent attachment relationship—until we look at peer interaction data using similar approaches. Then we find that not only is AAI security also strongly linked to adolescents' behavior with their peers, but that if anything, links to security appear to be stronger for behavior with peers than for behavior with parents (Allen, Porter, McFarland, McElhaney, & Marsh, in press). So, yes, adolescent states of mind are linked to behaviors with parents, but clearly this behavioral link is not at all restricted to primary attachment relationships.

PERSPECTIVE SHIFT 3. *Adolescent attachment states of mind may not even be directly assessing adolescent attachment behavioral systems.*

Ultimately our adolescent perspective requires us to revisit our starting point: the validation data demonstrating links from parental AAI classifications to the attachment behavior in the Strange Situation of their infant offspring (for a review of these studies, see van IJzendoorn, 1995). And here too, once we begin to carefully separate measure from construct, a critical distinction emerges. When conceptualized precisely, the parental AAI–infant Strange Situation studies do not provide direct evidence that the AAI is tapping into the parent's attachment system. Rather, what these studies show most directly is that the AAI is tapping into the parent's *caregiving* system. The one thing we know with striking clarity from these studies is that the mothers, including adolescent mothers, who are found to have autonomous states of mind regarding attachment in the AAI are able to provide care to their infants such that the infants (not the parents) ultimately behave in a secure fashion. This is not to say that other inductive or theoretical arguments do not suggest a link between the AAI and the parents' own attachment system. Rather, the point here is that the remarkable data provided by the AAI–Strange Situation studies are not in and of themselves sufficient to support the conclusion that the AAI is assessing the adolescent's or adult's attachment system, and in fact they point in a slightly different direction.

On theoretical grounds, we might of course expect considerable overlap between the attachment and caregiving systems, but clearly the two are not isomorphic. There is a deceptively large conceptual leap from observing the concordance of parent AAIs and infant Strange Situations to viewing the AAI as a marker of adult attachment. There is no logically a priori reason that a construct that predicts the attachment status of one's offspring necessarily directly reflects one's own attachment status in other relationships, particularly given the significant distinction between serving as a caregiver to one's offspring versus being a recipient of care in having one's needs met in other relationships. It is far more parsimonious simply to begin with the observation that Mary Main discovered a remarkably powerful way to use interviews to tap critical aspects of the caregiving system. It then becomes an open empirical question—and one highly worthy of study—to examine the extent to which the parental caregiving system is related to that parent's attachment system and attachment relationships.

Main and others have described the AAI as capturing an aspect of the attachment behavioral system: the internal organization of thinking and feelings regarding attachment behavior (Hesse, 1999; Main, 1999). Main has noted that this is nevertheless not the same as stating that what is seen in the AAI *is* the attachment system, and she carefully labels the resulting classifications from the AAI as "states of mind" regarding attachment. These states of mind parallel, but are not considered identical to, corresponding classifications of infant-parent attachments from the Strange Situation. Being a highly competent caregiver is not necessarily the same as being secure regarding one's own attachment needs. Knowing that the two systems are related (even strongly related) is not sufficient to call them identical.

But is this a difference that makes a difference? Yes, in all likelihood. For perhaps the AAI does not yield a direct translation of the kind of attachment behavior observed in infancy in specific relationships. Perhaps it captures something far more generalized. After all, classifications from the AAI have been related to a wide array of adolescent outcomes, from depression to delinquency to peer relationship quality (Adam, Sheldon-Keller, & West, 1996; Allen, Moore, Kuperminc, & Bell, 1998; Allen et al., in press; Bernier, Larose, & Whipple, 2005; Cole-Detke & Kobak, 1996; Kobak & Cole,

1994; Kobak, Sudler, & Gamble, 1991; Larose & Bernier, 2001; McElhaney, Immele, Smith, & Allen, 2006; Wallis & Steele, 2001). Perhaps the AAI is capturing an affect regulation process that is broader and more evolved than the infant's organization of attachment behavior with a caregiver. And perhaps it is not only our assessments that have broadened with development; perhaps infant attachment behavior and the attachment system itself have ultimately evolved into something more complex and far reaching as the organism has developed into adolescence.

Manifestations of Attachment Processes in Adolescence

From Safety and Survival to Affect Regulation. If we are to understand the ways in which attachment processes are actually manifest in adolescence, we must begin by recognizing the fundamental transformation that occurs from infancy to adolescence as the attachment behavioral system potentially evolves into a broader affect regulation system. Just as a seed pod changes dramatically as it matures into a developed plant, so too is the attachment behavioral system likely to look and be quite different in adolescence than in infancy.

In infancy, the attachment behavioral system plays a fundamental role in promoting the infant's physical survival. Survival and affect regulation are tightly linked in that the infant is likely to be most distressed (that is, most dysregulated) when experiencing conditions such as danger, hunger, or illness that are potentially linked to survival threats. As we move toward adolescence, the frequency of true survival threats diminishes greatly, but the importance of using social interactions to regulate affect remains. Except under extreme circumstances, adolescents generally do not need their attachment figures for safety regulation, but they do routinely need and use them to regulate their emotions.

In fact, much evidence suggests that this predisposition to regulate emotion through social relationships is as hardwired in adulthood as is attachment behavior in infancy and that the same wiring may be used for both. In other species, the formation of tight social bonds has been linked to reproductive fitness and survival of one's offspring (Silk, Alberts, & Altmann, 2003). In humans, meta-analyses indicate that a lack of adult social bonds creates a greater risk of future mortality than does cigarette smoking (House, Landis, & Umberson, 1988). On a neural level, Coan and others have pointed out that the systems responsible for maintenance of attachment appear to be virtually identical to those responsible for affect regulation (Coan, Schaefer, & Davidson, 2006; Hofer, 2006). Furthermore, Coan notes that evolutionary theorists dating to Darwin have argued that because mammalian emotional responding evolved in a social context, emotional behavior is virtually inextricable from social behavior (Brewer & Caporael, 1990;

Buss & Kenrick, 1998; Darwin & Ekman, 1872/1998). Thus, it appears likely that attachment behavior and affect regulation will be tightly linked over the course of the human life span.

Recognizing both the similarities and the distinctions between the precisely defined attachment behaviors of infancy and the broader affect regulation processes of adolescence has the advantage of allowing us to begin to spell out the mechanisms by which the two are connected. The attachment behavioral system, in addition to its primary survival functions, is likely to directly facilitate the infant's developing capacity for affect regulation and broader social bonding (Cassidy, 1994). At the same time, attachment behaviors may be conceptualized as specific instances of broader, developing affect regulation strategies. Yet well beyond infancy, these strategies are likely to be influenced by prior memories of infant experiences turning to attachment figures to manage both affect and survival goals.

In sum, we believe it is possible to view attachment behavior as distinct from but also as a precursor to broader patterns of social affect regulation. Although safety and survival obviously retain their primacy across the life span, on a practical basis, by adolescence the number of situations in which proximity to an attachment figure is required to maintain safety and survival has become vanishingly small. This is not to say that the attachment system does not remain operative, only that its primary purpose in infancy no longer has the same functional import by adolescence. In contrast, what some may consider to be more of a by-product of infant attachment behavior—learning to regulate affect in and through social interactions—becomes a central task of adolescent and adult functioning.

From Attachment to Affect Regulation: Reconciling Existing Findings. It is possible to array existing assessments on a continuum from pure attachment behaviors to assessments likely to tap broader affect regulation processes (see Figure 2.1). This continuum progresses from the infant Strange Situation, which assesses pure attachment behavior at one end, through assessments that blend elements of attachment behavior and affect regulation, to performance on the AAI, which we can now view as involving management of strong affect (albeit related to attachment memories) in the context of a discussion with an interviewer.

What is striking about this continuum is that where an assessment falls along it corresponds perfectly to the magnitude of its correlation to overall classifications of security in the AAI. The infant Strange Situation has some of the weakest concordances with the adolescent AAI (although it is also furthest removed in time). Current adolescent affect regulation with parents, as assessed in both conflict and support tasks, has been more strongly linked to the AAI (Allen et al., 2003; Kobak, Cole, Ferenz-Gillies, Fleming, & Gamble, 1993). Managing affect in peer relationships—in which the task is not simply using others for support (closer to tightly defined attachment behavior) but also being responsive to the emotional needs of others (closer to a

Figure 2.1. The Attachment–Affect Regulation Continuum

The Attachment—Affect Regulation Continuum

Tightest Focus
on Attachment-
Specific Behavior

Broadest Focus
on Affect
Regulation

Infant
Strange-
Situation

Affect
Regulation
in Adolescent-
Parent Interactions

Affect
Regulation
in Adolescent-
Peer Interactions

Affect
Regulation
During
Caregiving

Affect
Regulation
During
the AAI

Weakest
Correlation

Correlation with Adolescent Autonomous State of Mind
in the Adult Attachment Interview

Strongest
Correlation

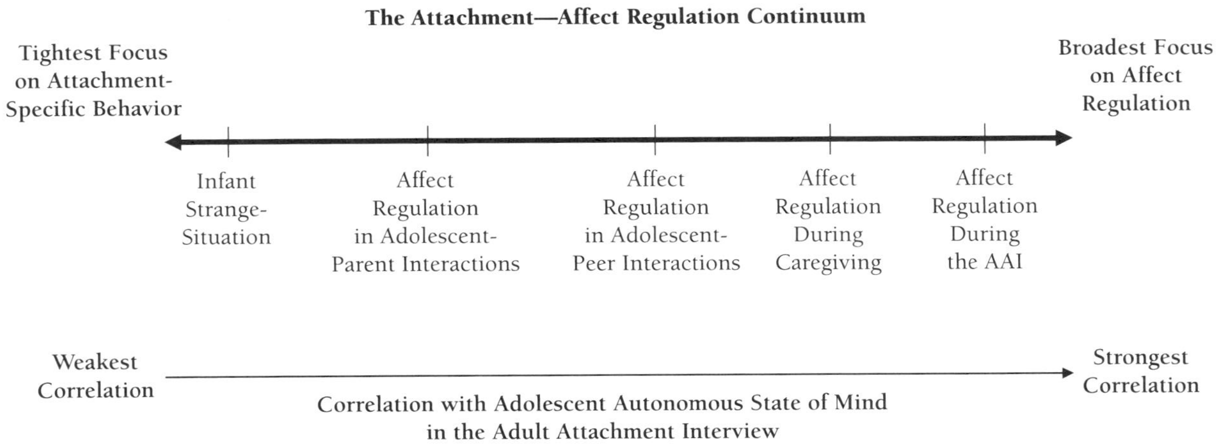

broad capacity to manage affect)—appears to have an even stronger connection to adolescent responses in the AAI (Allen et al., in press). And the strongest links to the AAI appear to be to the caregiving behaviors that lead one's offspring to be secure in the Strange Situation—behaviors that involve little or no receipt of help managing one's own safety needs, but rather being sufficiently capable of self-regulating one's own affect as to be able to consistently meet the needs of another individual (to function in terms of caregiving rather than care receiving). Notably, even within this continuum, we find that assessments that lie closer to one another also tend to display the strongest connections. Thus, we have reports from the Grossmans' lab that infant Strange Situation behavior is more strongly correlated with future autonomy negotiations with parents in adolescence, an affect-regulation paradigm with attachment figures, than with adolescent AAI security, an affect-regulation paradigm with parents absent (Zimmermann et al., 2000). Similarly, we find that affect regulation with parents is a stronger predictor of affect regulation with peers than is AAI security (Allen et al., in press).

If we want to find the strongest predictions from prior infant attachment behavior, we are likely to have the greatest success when examining areas of adolescent and adult functioning that reflect actual attachment behavior with attachment figures. From this perspective, the modest reported concordances between Strange Situation and later AAI assessments are not surprising and may not simply reflect intervening environmental events. Rather, this lack of strong concordance may in part reflect the substantial conceptual distance between an assessment of a relationship with a tight focus on attachment behavior versus an assessment of an intrapsychic characteristic that is more broadly focused on patterns of affect regulation.

None of this is to claim that the AAI is not tapping into attachment processes or that the only function of attachment beyond infancy is its contribution to affect regulation. Rather, this is to say that it is an open question as to whether what the AAI assesses is highly specific to the memories of the past attachment experiences on which it focuses or whether the underlying construct might also be almost equally well viewed in terms of broader patterns of affect regulation. We know that other AAI-like interviews tackling slightly different domains of behavior, such as the Current Relationship Interview and the Parent Development Interview (Aber, Belsky, Slade, & Crnic, 1999; Slade, Belsky, Aber, & Phelps, 1999; Slade, Slade, Grienenberger, Bernbach, Levy, & Locker, 2005; Treboux, Crowell, & Waters, 2004), are substantially but far from perfectly correlated with the AAI and demonstrate significant relations to other indicators of social-affective functioning. A critical unanswered question is the extent to which these observed patterns of adult affect regulation across different domains are relatively discrete versus overlapping.

Nor does stating that attachment in the Strange Situation and states of mind assessed in the AAI are distinct constructs mean they are unrelated. On the contrary, the organization of the attachment behavioral system undoubtedly contributes tremendously to general affect regulation capacities, as numerous researchers have now begun to document (Cassidy, 1994; Kobak et al., 1993; Kobak, Ferenz-Gillies, Everhart, & Seabrook, 1994; Mikulincer, 1998; Shaver & Mikulincer, 2002; Thompson, Flood, & Lundquist, 1995). This perspective suggests that there is likely to be tremendous value in examining the ways in which the organization of the attachment behavioral system in infancy becomes generalized beyond individual attachment relationships to affect far broader patterns of social affect regulation (Zimmermann, Maier, Winter, & Grossmann, 2001). Attachment theorists (Sroufe, Carlson, Levy, & Egeland, 1999) have rightfully been wary of claiming that attachment "explains everything" about human social behavior. And yet it is our view that a careful construction of the evolution of attachment processes will allow us to explore the ways in which attachment experiences evolve into lifelong patterns of affect regulation, within and beyond attachment relationships—that are in fact incredibly far reaching.

The Continuing Role of Relationships

Viewing the AAI as capturing one aspect of affect regulation also brings into sharp relief a major unanswered question: What about actual attachment relationships during this period? The AAI is an exquisitely sensitive instrument that has transformed the field. But to ask of an instrument that assesses an intrapsychic construct that it replace and obviate instruments that capture dyadic phenomena is to invite frustration. We next consider the ways in which an adolescent perspective suggests a need to consider both the increasing flexibility and greater complexity of adolescent relationships that serve attachment functions.

"Minor" Attachment Relationships. Infants typically have a limited number of caretakers not of their choosing. Adolescents, in contrast, can develop and select individuals to help them manage difficult emotional situations from among a wide range of candidates, including parents, teachers, relatives, close friends, romantic partners, and therapists. Furthermore, adolescents have a capacity to flexibly move into and out of such relationships. Even young adolescents appear to have the capacity to fully engage same-age peers as quasi-attachment figures for significant periods of time around certain issues. Adolescents may turn to a specific peer for comfort when distressed, feel freer exploring new behaviors in the presence of that peer, find the peer (at least for a time) irreplaceable, seek proximity with the peer, mourn the loss of the peer, and expect the peer to "be there" to meet their needs into the future (however foreshortened this future may be given an adolescent's present-oriented perspective). These comprise all of the formal criteria that have been described for identifying attachment relationships (Ainsworth, 1989; Cassidy, 1999). Such relationships occur with sufficient frequency that they are often topics of popular literature and well described within it (see Hinton, 1967; Evans, Gideon, Sheinman, A., & Reiner, 1986), and we may be fascinated with them precisely because they represent the developing human's first foray into recreating the power of the attachment system in new relationships with peers.

Whether we are willing to call these relationships "attachment relationships" appears in some respects as a matter of semantics. Our own inclination is to highlight the links to attachment behavior in these intensive peer interactions while continuing to draw distinctions between these interactions and primary attachment relationships. The real issue is that whatever we may call them, these relationships serve many, many attachment functions—providing felt security, affect regulation, and perhaps even actual safety—and they warrant understanding as such. The eventual development of a new primary attachment figure is of great interest and probably bears most continuity with attachment-related experiences with parents in infancy and childhood. But the capacity to adopt others as secondary, or what we might call "minor," attachment figures—sometimes for long periods of the life span in modest ways, sometimes only for very brief periods in intense ways (for example an eighteen-year-old soldier's comrade on a battlefield)—is also of potentially great importance. In infancy, these minor figures can be overlooked, perhaps at little cost. In adolescence and adulthood, they may become crucial. How else can we explain the healthy single mother able to raise secure offspring under often stressful circumstances, relying largely on an ensemble of what we may refer to as bit-part players in meeting her own attachment needs?

The Complexity of Attachment Relationships Beyond Childhood. Even full-fledged attachment relationships are likely to be radically different in adolescence than in infancy, for with increasing maturity, the attachment functions of relationships are going to become inextricably interwoven with other functions. In infancy, we mostly see an infant and parent both with the goal of trying to meet the infant's needs. In adolescence and adulthood, we have two individuals, each vying to get his or her own needs met simultaneously in the same relationship. For example, a relationship in which one individual provides a consistent, reliable secure base for the attachment needs of the other—and never expects the other to reciprocate—describes a quite healthy parent-infant relationship and a quite unhealthy teen friendship.

Clearly, if we want to understand adolescent and adult attachment relationships we will need to move from the A's, B's, and C's of infant classifications not simply to the D's, E's, and F's of intrapsychic measures regarding attachment but to a more complex language to capture the range and variety of adolescent and adult dyadic relationships. Even the simple number of permutations of attachment states of mind grows geometrically when considering dyads as opposed to individuals. What happens, for example, when an individual with a dismissing state of mind regarding attachment becomes involved in an intense relationship with an individual with a preoccupied or secure state of mind? Intriguing research has begun to tackle these questions (Cowan & Cowan, 2001; Crowell & Treboux, 2001; Paley, Cox, Burchinal, & Payne, 1999; Treboux et al., 2004), but far more remains to be done.

Power differentials also become important. Adolescents in particular are understandably reluctant to "depend" on another figure as "older and wiser," to use Bowlby's term, if this means giving up a degree of power and autonomy in future conflicts. Hence, adolescents may turn less to their parents as attachment figures not simply because they need them less to self-regulate but to avoid ceding power to them. It is unarguably more difficult to challenge a parent's authority after crying on his or her shoulder about a hard day at school. From this perspective, what might at first seem like an attachment conundrum—why an adolescent under stress might deliberately pull away from his or her primary attachment figures and refuse to communicate with them—becomes readily comprehensible. Power issues are not just superimposed on attachment behaviors; rather, they can fundamentally alter the expression of such behaviors.

These are just a few of the myriad ways in which attachment behaviors will ultimately be shaped and modified by other competing needs as the individual moves into adolescent and adult relationships. Other significant factors, such as gender, the influence of the mating system, and societal expectations of adult independence, all come to play an increasing role in how attachment behavior will be expressed. As close relationships develop beyond adolescence, security as assessed by the AAI clearly will play an important role in how these relationships develop and will influence other behavioral systems just as it is influenced by them (Furman, Simon, Shaffer, & Bouchey, 2002; Treboux et al., 2004). Indeed, at some point, the workings of the attachment behavioral system may become so tightly interwoven with that of other systems (affect regulation, reproductive, and parenting, for example) that it may make sense to reconfigure our thinking about adult behavioral systems in ways that better capture this complexity.

Future Directions

Additional research is clearly needed to advance our understanding of attachment in adolescence and beyond. Much of the discussion in this chapter, for example, presumes that the patterns of affect regulation observed in the AAI would bear at least some similarity to patterns of affect regulation in other situations that elicit strong emotion and involve intense interpersonal interaction. Research has begun to address this question by comparing AAI classifications to results of interviews targeting adolescent and adult romantic partners, although at least in adulthood, these are still potentially attachment relationships being assessed (Furman et al., 2002; Treboux et al., 2004).

Going further along these lines, efforts to assess strong affective situations that arise as a parent have also been developed, such as the Parent

Development Interview (Aber et al., 1999; Slade et al., 1999), and have more potential for exploring the true generality of what is observed in the AAI to assessments in which the individual's own attachment experiences are not the primary focus. Obviously a built-in confound will always exist in that the situations most likely to generate strong affect are typically going to be those involving human interaction, often with attachment figures. But to the extent that assessments of affect regulation patterns can be assessed using data other than memories of past attachment experiences, this is likely to advance our understanding not only of precisely what the AAI is assessing, but also of the broader links between individuals' organization of their thinking regarding attachment and their patterns of affect regulation.

Similarly, affect regulation may occur in both contexts that are closer to attachment-relevant situations and other situations that are more distal. We might expect, for example, that affect regulation in instances in which survival is threatened (for example, around serious illnesses) might more closely resemble prior attachment behavior than strong affect around less threatening situations. If we can begin to map out ways in which patterns of affect regulation do and do not display continuity across these contexts, we will have gone a significant distance toward developing a theory that can flesh out the ways in which the attachment behavioral system contributes to, is affected by, and yet remains distinct from a broader affect regulation system.

Finally, the development of our understanding of attachment as a life span phenomenon seems most likely to be enhanced by a continued effort to move beyond the intrapsychic assessment of attachment processes to assessing actual relationship behavior. This chapter has suggested that it is possible, and indeed desirable, to tap into critical aspects of the attachment and affect regulation systems in adolescence by assessing relationships (for example, with close peers) that are not typically considered full-fledged attachment relationships. Research that begins to identify ways that patterns of relating to peers mirror and diverge from patterns of relating to parental attachment figures can help begin to flesh out the nature of the connections between these two types of relationships.

Final Thoughts

In keeping with Freud and Bowlby's recognition of the need to continually expand our points of view, we offer in this chapter one such additional point of view regarding attachment as a life span phenomenon. We are obviously not proposing it as *the* correct point of view, but only as an alternative perspective on a remarkably complex phenomenon. We see nothing intrinsically wrong with the infant-centric view of attachment that has evolved as the field has grown from its infant origins. Quite to the contrary, this prior work has produced an incredibly rich and fertile ground of research and theory from which new ideas can grow and develop. Yet if we do not also examine the attachment system from completely different perspectives, we risk losing sight of the distinction between what is unique to childhood and what is unique to attachment processes across the life span.

Infancy shows us one facet of the attachment behavioral system—perhaps the most important facet—in a form that is dramatic and readily observable. But infancy is likely to provide too narrow a base on which to build an understanding of attachment across the life span. It is, of course, possible that an attachment homunculus persists inside the individual relatively unchanged throughout the life span—perhaps shifting in orientation (for example, from insecure to secure or vice versa) but retaining its fundamental form as new experiences accumulate. But it appears at least equally likely that the attachment system in infancy is more like a river that flows into the larger waters of affect regulation capacities as development progresses. We would argue that both existing data and analogies to other domains of human ontological development suggest that this second alternative merits serious consideration. Infants develop and become more complex and efficacious in their behavioral repertoires as they grow into maturity. Similarly, our theory of attachment is likely to become increasingly complex and powerful as it goes through its own process of maturation and growth in accounting for this development.

References

Aber, J. L., Belsky, J., Slade, A., & Crnic, K. (1999). Stability and change in mothers' representations of their relationship with their toddlers. *Developmental Psychology, 35,* 1038–1047.

Adam, K. S., Sheldon-Keller, A. E., & West, M. (1996). Attachment organization and history of suicidal behavior in clinical adolescents. *Journal of Consulting and Clinical Psychology, 64,* 264–272.

Ainsworth, M.D.S. (1989). Attachments beyond infancy. *American Psychologist, 44,* 709–716.

Allen, J. P., McElhaney, K. B., Land, D. J., Kuperminc, G. P., Moore, C. M., O'Beirne-Kelley, H., et al. (2003). A secure base in adolescence: Markers of attachment security in the mother-adolescent relationship. *Child Development, 74,* 292–307.

Allen, J. P., Moore, C., Kuperminc, G., & Bell, K. (1998). Attachment and adolescent psychosocial functioning. *Child Development, 69,* 1406–1419.

Allen, J. P., Porter, M. R., McFarland, F. C., McElhaney, K. B., & Marsh, P. A. (in press). The relation of attachment security to adolescents' paternal and peer relationships, depression, and externalizing behavior. *Child Development.*

Benoit, D., & Parker, K.C.H. (1994). Stability and transmission of attachment across three generations. *Child Development, 65,* 1444–1456.

Bernier, A., Larose, S., & Whipple, N. (2005). Leaving home for college: A potentially stressful event for adolescents with preoccupied attachment patterns. *Attachment and Human Development, 7,* 171–185.

Bowlby, J. (1969/1982). *Attachment and loss: Vol. 1.* New York: Basic Books.

Brewer, M. B., & Caporael, L. R. (1990). Selfish genes vs. selfish people: Sociobiology as origin myth. *Motivation and Emotion, 14,* 237–243.

Buss, D. M., & Kenrick, D. T. (1998). Evolutionary social psychology. *Handbook of Social Psychology, 2,* 982–1026.

Cassidy, J. (1994). Emotion regulation: Influences of attachment relationships. *Monographs of the Society for Research in Child Development, 59,* 228–283.

Cassidy, J. (1999). The nature of the child's ties. In J. Cassidy & P. R. Shaver (Eds.), *Handbook of attachment: Theory, research, and clinical applications* (pp. 3–20). New York: Guilford Press.

Coan, J. A., Schaefer, H. S., & Davidson, R. J. (2006). Lending a hand: Social regulation of the neural response to threat. *Psychological Science, 17,* 1032-1039.

Cole-Detke, H., & Kobak, R. (1996). Attachment processes in eating disorder and depression. *Journal of Consulting and Clinical Psychology, 64,* 282–290.

Cowan, P. A., & Cowan, C. P. (2001). A couple perspective on the transmission of attachment patterns. In C. Clulow (Ed.), *Adult attachment and couple psychotherapy: The "secure base" in practice and research* (pp. 63–82). New York: Brunner-Routledge.

Crowell, J., & Treboux, D. (2001). Attachment security in adult partnerships. In C. Clulow (Ed.), *Adult attachment and couple psychotherapy: The "secure base" in practice and research* (pp. 28–42). New York: Brunner-Routledge.

Darwin, C., & Ekman, P. (1872/1998). *The expression of the emotions in man and animals* (3rd ed.). New York: Oxford University Press.

Evans, B. A., Gideon, R., & Sheinman, A. (Producers), & Reiner, R. (Director). (1986). *Stand by me* [Motion picture]. United States: Columbia Pictures Company.

Freud, S. (1915). *Repression: The complete psychological works of Sigmund Freud.* London: Hogarth Press.

Furman, W., Simon, V. A., Shaffer, L., & Bouchey, H. A. (2002). Adolescents' working models and styles for relationships with parents, friends, and romantic partners. *Child Development, 73,* 241–255.

George, C., Kaplan, N., & Main, M. (1996). *Adult Attachment Interview* (3rd ed.). Unpublished manuscript, Department of Psychology, University of California, Berkeley.

Hamilton, C. E. (2000). Continuity and discontinuity of attachment from infancy through adolescence. *Child Development, 71,* 690–694.

Hesse, E. (1999). The Adult Attachment Interview: Historical and current perspectives. In J. Cassidy & P. R. Shaver (Eds.), *Handbook of attachment: Theory, research, and clinical applications* (pp. 395–433). New York: Guilford Press.

Hinton, S. E. (1967). *The outsiders.* New York: Viking Press.

Hofer, M. (2006). Psychobiological roots of early attachment. *Current Directions in Psychological Science, 15,* 84–88.

House, J. S., Landis, K. R., & Umberson, D. (1988). Social relationships and health. *Science, 241,* 540–545.

Kobak, R. R. (1990). *A Q-Sort system for coding the Adult Attachment Interview.* Unpublished manual, University of Delaware, Newark.

Kobak, R. R., & Cole, H. (1994). Attachment and meta-monitoring: Implications for adolescent autonomy and psychopathology. In D. Cicchetti & S. L. Toth (Eds.), *Disorders and dysfunctions of the self: Rochester Symposium on Developmental Psychopathology* (Vol. 5, pp. 267–297). Rochester, NY: University of Rochester Press.

Kobak, R. R., Cole, H., Ferenz-Gillies, R., Fleming, W., & Gamble, W. (1993). Attachment and emotion regulation during mother-teen problem-solving: A control theory analysis. *Child Development, 64,* 231–245.

Kobak, R. R., Ferenz-Gillies, R., Everhart, E., & Seabrook, L. (1994). Maternal attachment strategies and emotion regulation with adolescent offspring. *Journal of Research on Adolescence, 4,* 553–566.

Kobak, R. R., Sudler, N., & Gamble, W. (1991). Attachment and depressive symptoms during adolescence: A developmental pathways analysis. *Development and Psychopathology, 3,* 461–474.

Larose, S., & Bernier, A. (2001). Social support processes: Mediators of attachment state of mind and adjustment in late adolescence. *Attachment and Human Development, 3,* 96–120.

Main, M. (1999). Attachment theory: Eighteen points. In J. Cassidy & P. R. Shaver (Eds.), *Handbook of attachment: Theory, research, and clinical applications* (pp. 845–887). New York: Guilford Press.

Main, M., & George, C. (1985). Responses of abused and disadvantaged toddlers to distress in agemates: A study in the day care setting. *Developmental Psychology, 21,* 407–412.

Main, M., Goldwyn, R., & Hesse, E. (2002). *Adult Attachment scoring and classification systems, Version 7.1.* Unpublished manuscript, University of California at Berkeley.

Main, M., Kaplan, N., & Cassidy, J. (1985). Security in infancy, childhood, and adulthood: A move to the level of representation. In I. Bretherton & E. Waters (Eds.), Growing points in attachment theory and research. *Monographs of the Society for Research in Child Development, 50* (1–2, Serial No. 209), 66–106.

McElhaney, K. B., Immele, A., Smith, F. D., & Allen, J. P. (2006). Attachment organization as a moderator of the link between peer relationships and adolescent delinquency. *Attachment and Human Development, 8,* 33–46.

Mikulincer, M. (1998). Adult attachment style and individual differences in functional versus dysfunctional experiences of anger. *Journal of Personality and Social Psychology, 74,* 513–524.

Paley, B., Cox, M. J., Burchinal, M. R., & Payne, C. C. (1999). Attachment and marital functioning: Comparison of spouses with continuous-secure, earned-secure, dismissing, and preoccupied attachment stances. *Journal of Family Psychology, 13,* 580–597.

Shaver, P. R., & Mikulincer, M. (2002). Attachment-related psychodynamics. *Attachment and Human Development, 4,* 133–161.

Silk, J. B., Alberts, S. C., & Altmann, J. (2003). Social bonds of female baboons enhance infant survival. *Science, 302,* 1231–1234.

Slade, A., Belsky, J., Aber, J. L., & Phelps, J. L. (1999). Mothers' representations of their relationships with their toddlers: Links to adult attachment and observed mothering. *Developmental Psychology, 35,* 611–619.

Slade, A., Slade, A., Grienenberger, J., Bernbach, E., Levy, D., & Locker, A. (2005). Maternal reflective functioning, attachment, and the transmission gap: A preliminary study. *Attachment and Human Development, 7,* 283–298.

Sroufe, L. A., Carlson, E. A., Levy, A. K., & Egeland, B. (1999). Implications of attachment theory for developmental psychopathology. *Development and Psychopathology, 11,* 1–13.

Thompson, R. A., Flood, M. F., & Lundquist, L. (1995). Emotional regulation: Its relations to attachment and developmental psychopathology. In C. Dante, E. Sheree, & L. Toth (Eds.), *Emotion, cognition, and representation. Rochester symposium on developmental psychopathology* (Vol. 6, pp. 261–299). Rochester, NY: University of Rochester Press.

Treboux, D., Crowell, J. A., & Waters, E. (2004). When "new" meets "old": Configurations of adult attachment representations and their implications for marital functioning. *Developmental Psychology, 40,* 295–314.

van IJzendoorn, M. H. (1995). Adult attachment representations, parental responsiveness, and infant attachment: A meta-analysis on the predictive validity of the Adult Attachment Interview. *Psychological Bulletin, 117,* 387–403.

Wallis, P., & Steele, H. (2001). Attachment representations in adolescence: Further evidence from psychiatric residential settings. *Attachment and Human Development, 3,* 259–268.

Ward, M. J., & Carlson, E. A. (1995). Associations among adult attachment representations, maternal sensitivity, and infant-mother attachment in a sample of adolescent mothers. *Child Development, 66,* 69–79.

Waters, E., Merrick, S., Treboux, D., Crowell, J., & Albersheim, L. (2000). Attachment security in infancy and early adulthood: A twenty-year longitudinal study. *Child Development, 71,* 684–689.

Weinfield, N. S., Sroufe, L. A., & Egeland, B. (2000). Attachment from infancy to early adulthood in a high-risk sample: Continuity, discontinuity, and their correlates. *Child Development, 71,* 695–702.

Zimmermann, P., Becker-Stoll, F., Grossmann, K., Grossmann, K. E., Scheuerer-Englisch, H., & Wartner, U. (2000). Longitudinal attachment development from infancy through adolescence. *Psychologie in Erziehung und Unterricht, 47,* 99–117.

Zimmermann, P., Maier, M. A., Winter, M., & Grossmann, K. E. (2001). Attachment and adolescents' emotion regulation during a joint problem-solving task with a friend. *International Journal of Behavioral Development, 25,* 331–343.

JOSEPH P. ALLEN *is professor of psychology at the University of Virginia, Charlottesville, Virginia.*

NELL MANNING *is a doctoral student in psychology at the University of Virginia, Charlottesville.*

3

Do internal working models of attachment influence the ways in which adolescents process social information? The chapter addresses this intriguing question by reviewing studies that have examined links between attachment and adolescents' memory, feedback seeking, perceptions of others, and secure base scripts.

Attachment and the Processing of Social Information in Adolescence

Matthew J. Dykas, Jude Cassidy

A key proposition of attachment theory is that experience-based cognitive representations of attachment, often referred to as internal working models of attachment, influence the manner in which individuals process attachment-relevant social information (Bowlby, 1969/1982, 1973, 1980; Bretherton & Munholland, 1999; Main, Kaplan, & Cassidy, 1985). This proposition, once examined predominantly in studies of children and adults, has garnered a considerable amount of theoretical and empirical attention recently from researchers interested in studying the nature of adolescent attachment. This attention has led to new theoretical models and empirical studies, and the mounting data have lent support to the notion that adolescents' internal working models of attachment are linked to their processing of attachment-relevant social information. In the light of these recent developments, our goal in this chapter is to review this growing and important body of literature. We begin our review by discussing briefly the proposed structure and function of internal working models of attachment. This discussion focuses principally on internal working models' diverse social information processing properties and sets the stage for understanding how links between attachment and

Work on this chapter was supported in part by a postdoctoral research fellowship from the Family Research Laboratory, University of New Hampshire to Matthew J. Dykas (NIMH 5-T32-MH15161–25) and a grant from the National Institute for Child Health and Human Development to Jude Cassidy (RO1-HD36635).

NEW DIRECTIONS FOR CHILD AND ADOLESCENT DEVELOPMENT, no. 117, Fall 2007 © Wiley Periodicals, Inc.
Published online in Wiley InterScience (www.interscience.wiley.com) • DOI: 10.1002/cd.193

attachment-relevant social information processing emerge in adolescence. Next, we review empirical studies that have examined links between adolescent attachment and four aspects of information processing: memory, feedback seeking, perceptions of others, and secure base scripts. Finally, we end our review by providing general conclusions and several suggestions for future research. In this chapter, we focus on adolescents between the ages of thirteen and seventeen years.

Theoretical Background

According to attachment theory, internal working models of attachment emerge during infancy through repeated daily experiences with attachment figures (Bowlby, 1973). Although it is believed that infants often develop separate internal working models of attachment for mother, father, and other caregivers (see Ainsworth, 1982), these models function similarly to influence the manner in which infants obtain, organize, and operate on information found in their different attachment relationships (Bowlby, 1973, 1980; Bretherton & Munholland, 1999; Main et al., 1985). As articulated first in the writing of Bowlby (1973), a core function of these models is to store attachment-relevant social information that infants have obtained through their relational histories with attachment figures, such as information related to the degree to which the attachment figure has been available, responsive, and sensitive to the infant in times of need and distress—times when the infant's attachment system was activated (Bowlby, 1973). Attachment theorists believe this information is of particular importance because it contributes directly to whether infants develop either a secure or an insecure internal working model of attachment (Bowlby, 1973; see Belsky, 1999, for a review). Internal working models also function to help infants generate predictions regarding the ways in which their attachment figures will behave in subsequent attachment-related interactions (Bowlby, 1973; Thompson, 2006); infants then use these predictions to calibrate the attachment behavioral system. In addition, internal working models of attachment perform a variety of other functions, such as providing individuals with information about the self. According to Bowlby (1973), children will understand how acceptable or unacceptable they are in the eyes of an attachment figure and will in turn use this information to develop a complementary representation of the self as a person who is loved and valued (or not) by that figure.

Internal working models of attachment are thought to perform the same social information processing functions in adolescence that they performed in childhood. What is different, however, is that whereas children are thought to have separate internal working models of attachment for different caregivers, there is a growing consensus that these models consolidate into a single overarching attachment organization during adolescence (see also Chapter Five, this volume). Attachment theorists often refer to this single overarching attachment organization as a state of mind with respect to attachment (Main & Goldwyn, 1998; see Allen & Land, 1999, for a detailed account of this process). The emergence of a state of mind does not mean necessarily that adolescents lose their separate internal working models of attachment; indeed, as Allen and Land (1999) noted, "These distinctions (of representations between parents) may be clarified and sharpened during this period" (p. 320; see also Furman & Simon, 2004, for data that adolescents have separate states of mind for different attachment figures). However, the emergence of this state of mind does suggest that adolescents develop a generalized internal working model of attachment (that is, an internal working model of attachment not specific to a particular caregiver) that has evolved from specific attachment-related experiences with different caregivers (see Allen & Land, 1999, for a discussion of reasons why this state of mind is adaptive and may emerge in adolescence). Like adolescents' caregiver-specific internal working models of attachment, adolescents' state of mind with respect to attachment is believed to influence how they process attachment-relevant social information. More precisely, as Main and her colleagues (1985) suggested, adolescents' state of mind with respect to attachment provides individuals with conscious and unconscious rules "for the direction and organization of attention and memory, rules that permit or limit the individual's access to certain forms of knowledge regarding the self, the attachment figure, and the relationship between the self and the attachment figure" (p. 77).

To understand how adolescents' state of mind with respect to attachment might influence their processing of attachment-relevant social information, it is important to understand how this state of mind is assessed. Usually using the Adult Attachment Interview (AAI; George, Kaplan, & Main, 1984, 1985, 1996), attachment researchers tap adolescents' state of mind with respect to attachment through a series of questions designed to have adolescent interviewees give both general descriptions of their childhood relationships with their parents and specific memories in support of such descriptions. Interviewees classified as possessing a secure state of mind with respect to attachment demonstrate that they can attend to questions regarding their attachment experiences and can answer these questions in an open, thoughtful, and coherent manner, which suggests sufficient access to attachment-relevant memories. For example, secure adolescents provide specific memories that support the general descriptions that they use to describe their attachment relationships and show a capacity to freely explore thoughts and feelings related to both the positive and negative aspects of their attachment experiences (Hesse, 1999).

AAI interviewees classified as having an insecure state of mind with respect to attachment appear to defensively exclude or suppress (or both) attachment-relevant social information when answering questions during the AAI. Insecure-dismissing individuals, for example, exhibit especially limited access to attachment-related childhood memories and do not answer questions regarding their attachment experiences in an open, thoughtful, and coherent manner. They may state that their attachment relationships were

NEW DIRECTIONS FOR CHILD AND ADOLESCENT DEVELOPMENT • DOI: 10.1002/cd

generally positive (and may idealize such relationships), yet are unable to provide specific memories from childhood that would corroborate this sentiment. In fact, these individuals sometimes provide specific memories that contradict their positive assessments of their childhood attachment experiences. Other individuals in this group, however, derogate their attachment experiences, yet insist that their negative attachment-related experiences had no negative effect on them. Insecure-dismissing individuals may discuss their attachment experiences in these ways because their internal working models of attachment are limiting access to emotionally difficult and painful childhood memories (Cassidy & Kobak, 1988; Main et al., 1985).

In contrast, insecure-preoccupied adolescents show "uncontained" access to attachment-related childhood memories. Although these adolescents demonstrate the willingness to answer questions regarding their attachment-related childhood experiences, their answers demonstrate an angry, unobjective, or confused preoccupation with these experiences (Hesse, 1999). These adolescents often attend inappropriately to a specific question by focusing excessively on the details of particular childhood memories that have angered them. This excessive focus limits their capacity to provide an objective overview of the nature of their attachment relationships and the ways in which these experiences have influenced their development. It may be that insecure-preoccupied adolescents discuss their attachment-related experiences in this manner because their internal working models are diverting attention away from the individual's genuine memories of emotional pain and redirecting this attention to less damaging and less emotionally hurtful memories (Cassidy, 2005; Fosha, 2000).

An example of how a preoccupied state of mind might serve to shift attention comes from a recent AAI that we conducted with an adolescent girl in our laboratory. We asked her to provide a specific experience from childhood that would explain why she used the word *adversarial* to describe her childhood relationship with her mother. She talked at length for several minutes about how she and her mother had had an ongoing argument during the girl's childhood about whether she should wear a hat outside during cold weather. The girl talked in detail, yet in a relatively confused and unobjective manner, about why she did not feel she needed to wear a hat and why her mother felt (erroneously) that the girl needed to wear a hat. The girl became caught up, in a preoccupied and annoyed manner, with the details of justifying her side of the argument (including "scientific studies have conclusively proven . . .") and disdain about the faults of her mother's thinking. Despite two additional prompts for a specific incident, the girl was unable to provide one. Our proposal is that such a continuing focus on details of an argument serves to displace emotional reactions. That is, for insecure-preoccupied adolescents, it may be less distressing to discuss negative events of relative nonimportance (whether to wear a hat outside) than to acknowledge deeper issues of emotional distress stemming from negative attachment-related experiences.

The AAI has provided attachment researchers with valuable insight into how adolescents process information concerning their childhood attachment relationships and experiences. This instrument has also spurred considerable interest into how adolescents' internal working models of attachment might function to process other types of attachment-relevant information found in the social environment. A key prediction is that secure and insecure adolescents process this information differently and in ways that are congruent with how they process information during the AAI. Secure adolescents value attachment experiences and can discuss information related to these experiences coherently and objectively during the AAI. Therefore, secure adolescents should process other attachment-relevant social information coherently. Insecure adolescents have considerable difficulties discussing attachment-related experiences coherently during the AAI; similar difficulties, or biases, should emerge when insecure adolescents are presented with other attachment-relevant social information. We discuss these biases below.

In an attempt to explain why the same insecure individual may sometimes suppress negative information and sometimes focus on it, Cassidy (2005) proposed that the type of bias that emerges when insecure individuals process attachment-relevant social information may depend on the nature of the information itself. According to Bowlby (1980), if insecure individuals are processing attachment-relevant social information that could potentially activate the attachment system (for example, information related to parental lack of sensitivity, information related to poor childhood attachment experiences, or information about personal distress or vulnerability), insecure individuals' internal working models of attachment will function to implement rules that allow these individuals to filter this information from conscious awareness (that is, through defensive exclusion or suppression) so that it does not activate the attachment system and cause subsequent emotional distress. Yet, if insecure individuals are required to process attachment-relevant social information that does not acknowledge personal distress or that would not activate the attachment system, such as information related to the generic qualities of attachment figures, then, according to Cassidy (2005; see also Dykas & Cassidy, 2007a), insecure individuals' internal working models of attachment will function to process this information expeditiously. These individuals might, for example, process this information negatively because they will draw on previously existing negative attachment-related knowledge to process new information rapidly and efficiently so that they can deploy their mental resources elsewhere (see Bretherton & Munholland, 1999; see also Baldwin, 1992). Thus, during adolescence, information processing patterns may vary as a function of both the adolescent's attachment and the nature of the information.

Throughout this introductory section, we have used the phrase "attachment-relevant social information" to refer to information that should be processed (theoretically) by adolescents' internal working models of attachment. This phrase is intended to refer to information found within the context of attachment relationships (for example, information related to attachment figures, secure base and safe haven behavior, and separation and loss). Yet although internal working models of attachment are thought to function principally to process information related directly to attachment, these models also are thought to function to process at least some other social information as well, such as information that arouses adolescents' exploratory, affiliative, fear, or sexual behavioral systems (see Cassidy, 1999). For example, according to Bowlby (1973), attachment-related experiences, and the internal working models of attachment forged from them, tend to generalize to influence relationships with other persons (for example, siblings, peers, and strangers) that do not contain an attachment-related component (see also Berlin & Cassidy, 1999). It is believed, for example, that in the absence of information about other persons, adolescents will draw on knowledge about people they do know, such as attachment figures, to understand their relationships with these new persons (see also Chapter Six, this volume). Moreover, adolescents may process other environmental stimuli as a function of their attachment organization. Thus, according to this logic, it is conceivable that the rules that adolescents' internal working models of attachment employ to process attachment-related information will generalize—lawfully to some extent—to process other types of social information as well as nonsocial information. For instance, adolescents classified as insecure-dismissing on the AAI may also dismiss potentially painful information related to affiliative relationships like friendships. Relatedly, it may be that given the close links between the attachment and fear systems, adolescents who have developed attachment strategies characterized by heightened activation of the attachment system will attend and respond more quickly to the type of threatening environmental stimuli that serves to activate the attachment system. (Note that these arguments are similar to the more widespread notion held by developmentalists that individuals use existing cognitive structures in coming to understand new information; Piaget, 1954.)

Empirical Studies of Links Between Attachment and the Processing of Social Information

In this section, we review studies that have examined whether adolescent attachment and attachment-related representations are linked to four aspects of adolescents' processing of social information. Although (because of limited space) we focus exclusively on studies that have used the AAI to assess adolescent attachment, we note that there is also a large and important body of relevant work that has used "adult attachment style" measures to assess adolescent attachment (see Mikulincer & Shaver, 2007, for a review).

Memory. In one study that was designed to examine whether attachment models provide rules for the direction of memory, Feeney and Cassidy (2003) examined whether adolescents' representations of parents (as assessed using a battery of self-report measures linked empirically to the AAI;

Cassidy, Ziv, Feeney, Woodhouse, & Rodenberg, 2003) were linked to their revisionist memory for adolescent-parent conflict. (Revisionist memory refers to how a given event is remembered over time when memory for that specific event fades, making it necessary to "fill in the blanks" of forgotten information.) At time 1, adolescents engaged in a ten-minute laboratory discussion task about topics of conflict (for example, chores, using the family car, curfew) with their mothers and, separately, with their fathers. Immediately following each discussion, adolescents used a thirty-one-item questionnaire to rate their perceptions of the discussion; these items were then reduced (factor analytically) into summary scores reflecting how positive and negative the discussions were, as well as the degree to which adolescents felt they were treated with hostility by their parent. At time 2 (six weeks after time 1), the researchers asked adolescents to recall these discussions and to again rate their perceptions of the discussion using the same questionnaire.

Considered as a whole, results from both the initial study and a replication study indicated that adolescents revised their memory of the conflict discussions over time as a function of their representations of their parents. Adolescents who possessed more secure representations of their parents were more likely than other adolescents to remember the discussion as more positive and less negative than they had reported initially six weeks earlier; these adolescents also reported having received less hostile treatment than they had reported previously. These findings support the notion that as adolescents' memory for adolescent-parent interaction fades over time, adolescents who possess more secure representations of parents remember these interactions positively because their knowledge of their parents is positive generally. Adolescents with insecure representations, in contrast, remember these interactions negatively because their knowledge of their parents is negative generally. (See Dykas & Cassidy, 2007b, for related findings that the AAI classifications of these adolescents are linked to adolescent revisionist memory of interactions with both parents and peers.)

In another recent experimental investigation of attachment and memory, Dykas and Cassidy (2007b) examined whether adolescents' internal working models of attachment (as assessed using the AAI) were linked to their memory for childhood events. In this study, seventeen-year-old adolescents completed Mikulincer and Orbach's Childhood Memory Task (1995) which required adolescents to first recall emotionally significant memories from childhood, such as memories of sadness, and then to rate the emotional intensity of these memories, such as the degree to which they were sad during the memory of sadness. As expected, compared to their secure counterparts, adolescents classified as insecure on the AAI showed slower retrieval of emotionally significant childhood memories, a finding that supported the proposition that insecure adolescents' internal working models of attachment were functioning to limit access to these memories. However, a pair of mixed gender-related findings emerged, suggesting that boys and girls suppress the emotional intensity of these memories differently as a function of their internal working models of attachment. As expected, insecure girls had significantly less intense emotions than secure girls; yet contrary to expectations, insecure boys had significantly more intense emotions than secure boys. These gender-related findings might provide evidence that for insecure boys (but not girls), negative childhood memories are not distressing and are thus recalled rapidly and efficiently. Clearly, more work is needed in this area before any firm conclusions can be drawn, especially given that the aggregation of the insecure-dismissing and insecure preoccupied adolescents into one insecure group (due to sample size) restricted to some extent the ability to learn more regarding the distinctive way that dismissing and preoccupied adolescents process emotionally significant childhood memories.

Feedback Seeking. Data from another study suggest that adolescents' internal working models of attachment might guide the ways in which adolescents seek out information about the self (Cassidy, Ziv, Mehta, & Feeney, 2003). In this study, Cassidy and her colleagues told high school students that other students would be asked six questions about the target adolescent and that "because of time," the target adolescent could view the responses to only three of the six questions. Three of the possible questions indicated a desire for positive feedback (for example, "Why might this person be happy with himself or herself most of the time?"). The other three possible questions indicated a desire for negative feedback (for example, "Why would this person often wish he or she was different?"). Results indicated that as adolescents' positive perceptions of maternal acceptance increased, so did their desire to seek out positive information about the self. Moreover, results indicated that adolescents' degree of global self-worth meditated this link. According to Cassidy and her colleagues, these mediational findings were important because they supported the notion that attachment security contributes to the development of a positive representational model of self that, once created, guides the processing of information related to the self.

Perceptions of Others. Increasing evidence indicates that secure adolescents generally have more positive perceptions of attachment figures and other persons in their lives than do insecure adolescents. Studies that have used the AAI, for example, have reported that compared to insecure adolescents, secure adolescents have more positive perceptions of their parents (Allen et al., 2003; Cassidy et al., 2003; West, Rose, Spreng, Sheldon-Keller, & Adam, 1998). In one of these studies, Cassidy et al. (2003) reported that secure adolescents were more likely than insecure adolescents to perceive both their mothers and their fathers as secure bases and as understanding of their emotional needs and wishes. Secure adolescents were also less likely to perceive their parents as hostile and their mothers as psychologically controlling. In another study, Allen et al. (2003) found that greater adolescent attachment security was linked to more positive perceptions of maternal supportiveness, and fewer idealized perceptions of the childhood relationship with their mother (see also Allen, McElhaney, Kuperminc, & Jodl,

2004). Moreover, in the laboratory examination involving the adolescent-parent conflict discussion described above (Feeney & Cassidy, 2003), findings revealed associations between adolescents' positive representations of their parents and adolescents' perceptions provided immediately following the discussion that both their mothers and their fathers treated them with less hostility. Thus, across these studies, there is evidence that attachment and attachment-related representations are related to perceptions of attachment figures both globally and in relation to a specific interaction.

Studies using the AAI have also shown that security is associated with more positive perceptions of peers. Secure adolescents have been found to be more likely than insecure adolescents to have positive and flexible expectations of hypothetical peer rejection situations (Zimmermann, 1999) and more positive attributions of peer integration and friendships (Zimmermann, 2004). In a related study, Furman and his colleagues (Furman, Simon, Shaffer, & Bouchey, 2002) examined how adolescents' internal working models of attachment were linked to their working models and perceptions of peers and romantic partners. Using modified versions of the AAI to assess working models of peers and romantic partners, these researchers reported that significant concordance existed between adolescents' internal working models of attachment and their working models of peers (that is, secure, dismissing, and preoccupied adolescents were likely to possess working models of peers that were either secure, dismissing, or preoccupied, respectively). Significant links also emerged between adolescents' internal working models of attachment and their working models of romantic partners such that adolescents classified as either secure or preoccupied on the AAI had either secure or preoccupied working models of romantic partners, respectively (adolescents classified as dismissing on the AAI were not likely to have dismissing working models of romantic partners). Related self-report data also emerged indicating that adolescents perceived that relationship styles and experiences with parents, peers, and romantic styles were associated with each other. These studies, and those discussed in the previous paragraph, support the notion that adolescents draw on their internal working models of attachment to process information related to others and, in some cases, generalize their internal working models of attachment when processing information related to peers.

Secure Base Scripts. Finally, attachment researchers have begun to examine whether adolescents' capacities to construct a secure base script are associated with their internal working models of attachment. According to attachment theory, a secure base script is a mental casual-temporal prototype of the ways in which attachment-related events are likely to unfold (for example, "When I am hurt, I go to my mother and my mother, in turn, comforts me"; Waters, Rodrigues, & Ridgeway, 1998; see also Bretherton, 1991). Adolescents who can construct a secure base script articulate that they or other persons can successfully use attachment figures as a secure base from which to explore and as a safe haven to return to in time of need or distress (Waters et al., 1998). Recent studies have shown that although some adolescents can construct secure base scripts, others cannot (Dykas, Woodhouse, Cassidy, & Waters, 2006; Elliott, Tini, Fetten, & Saunders, 2003; Steiner, Arjomand, & Waters, 2003), and one recent study has linked adolescents' secure base scripts to their internal working models of attachment (Dykas et al., 2006). In this study, adolescents completed the Adolescent Script Assessment (Steiner et al., 2003), which was based on the original assessment used to examine secure base scripts in adults (Waters & Rodrigues-Doolabh, 2001). Using this assessment, the researchers presented adolescents with six sets of (mostly neutral) words and instructed them to generate six different stories using these words. Two sets of words each centered around a mother or a father, and the third set centered around two nonspecific others. Adolescents who exhibited greater coherence of mind in the AAI were more likely than other adolescents to have knowledge and access to secure base scripts regarding mothers, fathers, and adults. Secure adolescents, for example, generated scripts in which the story protagonist seeks proximity to a parent, receives comfort and support from that parent, and successfully reengages in exploration. Interestingly, although greater AAI coherence was linked to greater access to and knowledge of a secure base script for mothers, fathers, and adults, it was only knowledge and access to a mother script that uniquely predicted AAI coherence. It might be that because mothers are typically the principal attachment figures, adolescent attachment might have a particularly important association with how adolescents process information related to mother figures.

Summary and Future Directions

Bowlby (1973, 1980) proposed that attachment is linked to the ways in which individuals process social information, and the studies reviewed in this chapter provide evidence that these links exist in adolescents. Compared to adolescents who possess insecure internal working models, adolescents who possess secure internal working models demonstrate more open and flexible processing of social information, and unlike their insecure counterparts, they do not tend to suppress attachment-relevant social information. Although none of the studies reviewed here have been replicated, all are theory based and their findings are convergent with empirical examinations of children and adults (see Dykas & Cassidy, 2007a, for a review). Moreover, these studies examine, directly or indirectly, a variety of information processing dimensions and components found in larger models of adolescent social information processing (for example, Crick & Dodge, 1994). On the basis of this evidence, we believe that the study of adolescent attachment will gain much from future investigations that examine adolescents' attachment-relevant social information processing. In the remainder of this chapter, we identify and discuss several areas of future research that should be of interest to researchers.

Understanding whether adolescents' internal working models of attachment are linked to their attention to attachment-relevant social information is an important area for future research. To date, no published study has examined whether secure and insecure adolescents attend to attachment-relevant social information differently, despite the fact that all information must be attended to before it can be operated on, stored, and recalled by adolescents. Research with children and adults suggests that such differences would emerge. For example, compared to children with secure attachment histories, children with insecure attachment histories have had more limited attention to information concerning attachment figures and attachment-related events (for example, Main et al., 1985; Kirsh & Cassidy, 1997). Moreover, links between adults' AAI classifications and their attention to various types of attachment-relevant social information have emerged in several studies (for example, Maier et al., 2005; van Emmichoven, van IJzendoorn, de Ruiter, & Brosschot, 2003). On the basis of these findings, we encourage researchers to examine connections between attachment and attention in adolescence. We believe that such examinations will provide a more comprehensive picture of how social information is processed by secure and insecure adolescents.

Examining how secure and insecure adolescents interpret ambiguous social stimuli is also an important direction for future research. For example, if a person's actions cause distress or harm to an adolescent, are there attachment-related differences in the way that adolescents process this information, such that insecure adolescents are more likely than secure adolescents to attribute hostile intent? Research with children indicates that such negative biases are linked to insecure attachment (for example, Cassidy, Kirsh, Scolton, & Parke, 1996; Suess, Grossmann, & Sroufe, 1992). Cassidy et al. (1996), for example, reported that insecure attachment was linked both longitudinally and contemporaneously to children's negative attributions when responding to hypothetical stories (based on the work of Dodge & Frame, 1982) in which a peer clearly caused something negative to happen to the child, but the peer's intent and circumstances were ambiguous. Because such negative biases have been found to place individuals at risk for poorer social and emotional adjustment (see Crick & Dodge, 1994, for a review), it is important to understand whether these biases are associated with adolescents' internal working models of attachment.

Another important avenue for future research is the examination of whether attachment-relevant social information processing mediates or moderates, or both, links between attachment and different indicators of adolescent social and emotional adjustment. For example, although links have emerged between adolescent attachment and adolescents' behavior toward mother (for example, Allen et al., 2003; Kobak, Cole, Ferenz-Gillies, Fleming, & Gamble, 1993), father (Ziv, Dykas, Feeney, & Cassidy, 2007), best friends (for example, Zimmermann, Maier, Winter, & Grossmann, 2001), and peers (for example, Dykas, Ziv, & Cassidy, 2007), the mechanisms by which attachment influences behavior is not well understood. According to attachment theory, it is reasonable to believe that adolescents' information processing mediates this link, such that adolescents' internal working models of attachment guide the processing of attachment-relevant social information, and this information processing in turn influences the ways in which adolescents behave toward others (Bowlby, 1973). Empirical evidence in support of this mediational model has emerged in studies of young children (for example, Cassidy et al., 1996), and we feel that similar models should be explored in future adolescent attachment research. Examination of these models could shed light on how distal linkages emerge between mental representations of early attachment experiences and later behavior. Moreover, examination of these models could have important implications for clinical work. Knowledge of links among attachment, information processing, and behavior could assist clinicians in targeting inflexible or negatively biased information processing patterns that may lead insecure (and perhaps secure) adolescents to behave negatively toward other individuals.

In addition to examining mediational models, attachment researchers could examine whether attachment-relevant social information processing moderates connections between attachment and different social and emotional outcomes. Although links between internal working models of attachment and psychosocial functioning have emerged in several studies (see Allen & Land, 1999, for a review), the strength of this link varied across studies, and it is possible that social information processing patterns could account for this variation. For example, links between insecurity of attachment and depression could be amplified in adolescents who process attachment-relevant social information in a negatively biased manner (for example, insecure adolescents may be at greater risk for depression if they view others negatively). Insecure adolescents who process this information in a positively biased manner may be protected against depression. In future investigations, the examination of moderational models could increase understanding of how links between adolescent attachment and adjustment might be dependent on adolescents' internal cognitive processes.

Another direction for future research could be the examination of how links between attachment and social information processing in adolescence are similar to and different from those found during other developmental periods. Earlier in this chapter, we stated that internal working models of attachment likely perform the same social information processing functions in adolescence that they performed in childhood. Although this notion is rooted in attachment theory, researchers have yet to examine whether links between attachment and social information processing are indeed similar across childhood, adolescence, and adulthood. We speculate that there are several reasons that these links (although conceptually similar) may appear different across different ages. For example, from a physiological perspective, neural and synaptic development continues well into adolescence, and these changes in brain development might alter the nature of these connections across childhood and adolescence. Recent evidence has also emerged that substantial brain changes occur throughout adulthood (see Steven & Blakemore, 2004), and these changes may be related to differences in information processing between adolescents and adults. Similarly, cognition becomes more complex and intricate with age, and links between attachment and information processing might also become more complex with age. In adolescence, a number of salient and unique developmental tasks (such as achieving greater autonomy from one's parents and forming new romantic attachments; see Chapters One and Four, this volume) might also alter the apparent nature of links between attachment and social information processing. Although a challenge for future researchers is to develop methodologies to test differences among children, adolescents, and adults, longitudinal and cross-sectional studies would provide much needed insight into these areas of inquiry.

Finally, although this chapter has focused principally on the processing of attachment-relevant social information, we believe that future researchers should examine whether internal working models of attachment are connected to more general aspects of adolescent cognitive development (see Keating, 2004). Steinberg (2005) has noted that a relatively new direction in the study of adolescent cognitive development is the examination of how judgment, decision making, risk taking, and other cognitive processes are influenced by both social and emotional contextual factors. To our knowledge, no published studies have examined whether adolescents' internal working models of attachment affect their cognitive development, despite indirect (behavioral) evidence that insecure adolescents make poorer decisions and take greater risks than secure adolescents do (for example, Allen, Moore, Kuperminc, & Bell, 1998). Evidence that attachment is linked to different aspects of children's cognitive development, like theory of mind development (for example, McElwain & Volling, 2004; Meins, Fernyhough, Russell, & Clark-Carter, 1998; Symons & Clark, 2000), also lends support to the notion that attachment might be connected to adolescent cognitive development. In the future, adolescent attachment research could provide valuable insight into adolescent cognitive development and shed light on whether experiences within the family affect how the adolescent brain functions more broadly.

References

Ainsworth, M.D.S. (1982). Attachment: Retrospect and prospect. In C. M. Parkes & J. Stevenson-Hinde (Eds.), *The place of attachment in human behavior* (pp. 3–30). New York: Basic Books.

Allen, J. P., & Land, D. (1999). Attachment in adolescence. In J. Cassidy & P. R. Shaver (Eds.), *Handbook of attachment: Theory, research, and clinical applications* (pp. 319–335). New York: Guilford Press.

Allen, J. P., McElhaney, K. B., Kuperminc, G. P., & Jodl, K. M. (2004). Stability and change in attachment security across adolescence. *Child Development, 75,* 1792–1805.

Allen, J. P., McElhaney, K. B., Land, D. J., Kuperminc, G. P., Moore, C. W., O'Beirne-Kelly, H., et al. (2003). A secure base in adolescence: Markers of attachment security in the mother-adolescent relationship. *Child Development, 74,* 292–307.

Allen, J. P., Moore, C., Kuperminc, G., & Bell, K. (1998). Attachment and adolescent psychosocial functioning. *Child Development, 69,* 1406–1419.

Baldwin, M. W. (1992). Relational schemas and the processing of social information. *Psychological Bulletin, 112,* 461–484.

Belsky, J. (1999). Interactional and contextual determinants of attachment security. In J. Cassidy & P. R. Shaver (Eds.), *Handbook of attachment: Theory, research, and clinical applications* (pp. 249–264). New York: Guilford Press.

Berlin, L., & Cassidy, J. (1999). Relations among relationships: Contributions from attachment theory and research. In J. Cassidy & P. R. Shaver (Eds.), *Handbook of attachment: Theory, research, and clinical applications* (pp. 319–335). New York: Guilford Press.

Bowlby, J. (1969/1982). *Attachment and loss: Vol. 1. Attachment.* New York: Basic Books.

Bowlby, J. (1973). *Attachment and loss: Vol. 2. Separation.* New York: Basic Books.

Bowlby, J. (1980). *Attachment and loss: Vol. 3. Loss.* New York: Basic Books.

Bretherton, I. (1991). Pouring new wine into old bottles: The social self as internal working model. In M. Gunnar & L. A. Sroufe (Eds.), *Minnesota Symposia in Child Psychology: Self Processes in Development* (pp. 1–41). Mahwah, NJ: Erlbaum.

Bretherton, I., & Munholland, K. A. (1999). Internal working models in attachment relationships: A construct revisited. In J. Cassidy & P. R. Shaver (Eds.), *Handbook of attachment: Theory, research, and clinical applications* (pp. 89–111). New York: Guilford Press.

Cassidy, J. (1999). The nature of the child's ties. In J. Cassidy & P. R. Shaver (Eds.), *Handbook of attachment: Theory, research, and clinical applications* (pp. 3–20). New York: Guilford Press.

Cassidy, J. (2005, July). *Being open to the pain of a difficult past: Therapeutic implications.* Paper presented at the International Conference on Attachment, Faculté de Médecine Xavier Bichat, Paris.

Cassidy, J., Kirsh, S. J., Scolton, K. L., & Parke, R. D. (1996). Attachment and representations of peer relationships. *Developmental Psychology, 32,* 892–904.

Cassidy, J., & Kobak, R. R. (1988). Avoidance and its relation to other defensive processes. In J. Belsky & T. Nezworski (Eds.), *Clinical implications of attachment* (pp. 300–323). Mahwah, NJ: Erlbaum.

Cassidy, J., Ziv, Y., Feeney, B. C., Woodhouse, S. S., & Rodenberg, M. (2003, April). Adolescents' perceptions of parents: Associations with attachment (AAI) classification and interactions with parents. In R. Kobak (chair), *Assessing attachment in middle childhood and adolescence: Toward a multimethod approach.* Symposium conducted at the Biennial Meetings of the Society for Research in Child Development, Tampa, FL.

Cassidy, J., Ziv, Y., Mehta, T. G., & Feeney, B. C. (2003). Feedback seeking in children and adolescents: Associations with self-perceptions, attachment representations, and depression. *Child Development, 74,* 612–628.

Crick, N. R., & Dodge, K. A. (1994). A review and reformulation of social information-processing mechanisms in children's social adjustment. *Psychological Bulletin, 115,* 74–101.

Dodge, K. A., & Frame, C. (1982). Social cognitive biases and deficits in aggressive boys. *Child Development, 53,* 620–635.

Dykas, M. J., & Cassidy, J. (2007a). *The role of attachment in shaping cognitive-affective mechanisms for the processing of social information: Theory and evidence.* Manuscript in preparation.

Dykas, M. J., & Cassidy, J. (2007b). *Attachment and adolescents' memory for attachment-relevant social information.* Manuscript in preparation.

Dykas, M. J., Woodhouse, S. S., Cassidy, J., & Waters, H. S. (2006). Narrative assessment of attachment representations: Links between secure base scripts and adolescent attachment. *Attachment and Human Development, 8,* 221–240.

Dykas, M. J., Ziv, Y., & Cassidy, J. (2007). *Attachment and peer relations in adolescence.* Manuscript submitted for publication.

Elliott, M., Tini, M., Fetten, E., & Saunders, A. (2003, April). *Attachment scripts in adult and adolescent males.* Paper presented at the Biennial Meetings of the Society for Research in Child Development, Tampa, FL.

Feeney, B. C., & Cassidy, J. (2003). Reconstructive memory related to adolescent-parent conflict interactions: The influence of attachment-related representations on immediate perceptions and changes in perceptions over time. *Journal of Personality and Social Psychology, 85,* 945–955.

Fosha, D. (2000). *The transforming power of affect.* New York: Basic Books.

Furman, W., & Simon, V. A. (2004). Concordance in attachment states of mind and styles with respect to fathers and mothers. *Developmental Psychology, 40,* 1239–1247.

Furman, W., Simon, V. A., Shaffer, L., & Bouchey, H. A. (2002). Adolescents' working models and styles for relationships with parents, friends, and romantic partners. *Child Development, 73,* 241–255.

George, C., Kaplan, N., & Main, M. (1984). *Adult Attachment Interview Protocol.* Unpublished manuscript, University of California at Berkeley.

George, C., Kaplan, N., & Main, M. (1985). *Adult Attachment Interview Protocol* (2nd ed.). Unpublished manuscript, University of California at Berkeley.

George, C., Kaplan, N., & Main, M. (1996). *Adult Attachment Interview Protocol* (3rd ed.). Unpublished manuscript, University of California at Berkeley.

Hesse, E. (1999). The Adult Attachment Interview: Historical and current perspectives. In J. Cassidy & P. R. Shaver (Eds.), *Handbook of attachment: Theory, research, and clinical applications* (pp. 395–433). New York: Guilford Press.

Keating, D. P. (2004). Cognitive and brain development. In R. M. Lerner & L. Steinberg (Eds.), *Handbook of adolescent psychology* (2nd ed., pp. 45–84). Hoboken, NJ: Wiley.

Kirsh, S. J., & Cassidy, J. (1997). Preschoolers' attention to and memory for attachment-relevant information. *Child Development, 68,* 1143–1153.

Kobak, R. R., Cole, H. E., Ferenz-Gillies, R., Fleming, W. S., & Gamble, W. (1993). Attachment and emotion regulation during mother-teen problem-solving: A control theory analysis. *Child Development, 64,* 231–245.

Maier, M. A., Bernier, A., Pekrun, R., Zimmermann, P., Strasser, K., & Grossmann, K. E. (2005). Attachment working models as unconscious structures: An experimental test. *International Journal of Behavioral Development, 28,* 180–189.

Main, M., & Goldwyn, R. (1998). *Adult attachment rating and classification systems.* Unpublished manuscript, University of California at Berkeley.

Main, M., Kaplan, N., & Cassidy, J. (1985). Security in infancy, childhood, and adulthood: A move to the level of representation. In I. Bretherton & E. Waters (Eds.), Growing points in attachment theory and research. *Monographs of the Society for Research in Child Development, 50* (1–2, Serial No. 209), 66–106.

McElwain, N. L., & Volling, B. L. (2004). Attachment security and parental sensitivity during infancy: Associations with friendship quality and false-belief understanding at age four. *Journal of Social and Personal Relationships, 21,* 639–667.

Meins, E., Fernyhough, C., Russell, J., & Clark-Carter, D. (1998). Security of attachment as a predictor of symbolic and mentalising abilities: A longitudinal study. *Social Development, 7,* 1–24.

Mikulincer, M., & Orbach, I. (1995). Attachment styles and repressive defensiveness: The accessibility and architecture of affective memories. *Journal of Personality and Social Psychology, 68,* 917–925.

Mikulincer, M., & Shaver, P. R. (2007). *Attachment in adulthood: Structure, dynamics, and change.* New York: Guilford Press.

Piaget, J. (1954). *The child's construction of reality.* New York: Basic Books.

Steinberg, L. (2005). Cognitive and affective development in adolescence. *Trends in Cognitive Sciences, 9,* 69–74.

Steiner, M. C., Arjomand, M., & Waters, H. S. (2003, April). *Adolescents' representations of close relationships.* Paper presented at the Biennial Meetings of the Society for Research in Child Development, Tampa, FL.

Steven, M. S., & Blakemore, C. (2004). Cortical plasticity in the adult human brain. In M. S. Gazzaniga (Ed.), *The cognitive neurosciences* (3rd ed., pp. 1243–1254). Cambridge, MA: MIT Press.

Suess, G. J., Grossmann, K. E., & Sroufe, L. A. (1992). Effects of infant attachment to mother and father on quality of adaptation in preschool: From dyadic to individual organisation of self. *International Journal of Behavioral Development, 15,* 43–65.

Symons, D. K., & Clark, S. E. (2000). A longitudinal study of mother-child relationships and theory of mind in the preschool period. *Social Development, 9,* 3–23.

Thompson, R. A. (2006). The development of the person: Social understanding, relationships, conscience, self. In N. Eisenberg (Ed.), W. Damon, & R. Lerner (Series Ed.), *Handbook of child psychology: Vol. 3. Social, emotional, and personality development* (6th ed., pp. 24–98). Hoboken, NJ: Wiley.

van Emmichoven, I.A.Z., van IJzendoorn, M. H., de Ruiter, C., & Brosschot, J. F. (2003). Selective processing of threatening information: Effects of attachment representation and anxiety disorder on attention and memory. *Development and Psychopathology, 15,* 219–237.

Waters, H. S., & Rodrigues-Doolabh, L. (2001, April). *Are attachment scripts the building blocks of attachment representations?* Paper presented at the Biennial Meetings of the Society for Research in Child Development, Minneapolis, MN.

Waters, H. S., Rodrigues, L. M., & Ridgeway, D. (1998). Cognitive underpinnings of narrative attachment assessment. *Journal of Experimental Child Psychology, 71,* 211–234.

West, M., Rose, S., Spreng, S., Sheldon-Keller, A., & Adam, S. (1998). Adolescent Attachment Questionnaire: A brief assessment of attachment in adolescence. *Journal of Youth and Adolescence, 27,* 661–673.

Zimmermann, P. (1999). Structure and functions of internal working models of attachment and their role for emotion regulation. *Attachment and Human Development, 1,* 291–306.

Zimmermann, P. (2004). Attachment representations and characteristics of friendship relations during adolescence. *Journal of Experimental Child Psychology, 88,* 83–101.

Zimmermann, P., Maier, M. A., Winter, M., & Grossmann, K. E. (2001). Attachment and adolescents' emotion regulation during a joint problem-solving task with a friend. *International Journal of Behavioral Development, 25,* 331–343.

Ziv, Y., Dykas, M. J., Feeney, B. C., & Cassidy, J. (2007). *Parental secure base provision and adolescent secure base use: Relations with adolescent attachment security.* Manuscript under review.

MATTHEW J. DYKAS is a postdoctoral research fellow at the Family Research Laboratory, University of New Hampshire.

JUDE CASSIDY is professor of psychology and director of the Maryland Child and Family Development Laboratory at the University of Maryland, College Park.

4

Puberty alters the interplay of attachment, sexual, and affiliative systems; initiates the search for a peer attachment; and begins the reorganization of adolescents' attachment hierarchies

Adolescent Attachment Hierarchies and the Search for an Adult Pair-Bond

Roger Kobak, Natalie L. Rosenthal, Kristyn Zajac, Stephanie D. Madsen

Adolescence begins with puberty and the emergence of the sexual behavioral system (Ainsworth, 1989). This development alters the dynamic interplay with well-established attachment and affiliative systems and works to reorganize adolescents' involvement with parents and peers (that is, friends and romantic partners). In Western industrial societies, the relatively long delay between onset of puberty and childbearing creates a lengthy and gradual transition to adult reproductive and caregiving roles. Initially sexual and affiliative systems work in synchrony to increase teens' emotional involvement in peer relationships. Time spent with friends and romantic partners creates new opportunities for developing the competencies required for the longer-term tasks of forming adult pair-bonds (Connolly, Furman, & Konarski, 2000). During this period, most teens maintain attachment bonds to parents while testing peers as sources of safety and support. Despite adolescents' use of peers to serve secure base and safe haven functions, most friendships or romantic relationships will not become enduring attachment bonds (Ainsworth, 1989). As a result, bonds with a romantic partner or close friend are not usually formed until late adolescence and only after a relationship has lasted for more than two years (Hazan & Zeifman, 1994; Trinke & Bartholomew, 1997).

This chapter was completed with the assistance of a grant from the National Institute of Mental Health (RO1-MH59670).

NEW DIRECTIONS FOR CHILD AND ADOLESCENT DEVELOPMENT, no. 117, Fall 2007   © Wiley Periodicals, Inc.
Published online in Wiley InterScience (www.interscience.wiley.com) • DOI: 10.1002/cd.194

In this chapter, we explore how Bowlby's concept of a hierarchy of attachment figures (1969/1982) can advance understanding of adolescent attachment relationships. More specifically, we believe that the concept of attachment hierarchies can lead to a better understanding of (1) whom adolescents identify as attachment figures; (2) when peer relationships are transformed to attachment bonds; (3) how adolescents organize multiple attachment bonds with parents, friends, and romantic partners; and (4) how attachment bonds are reorganized as friends and romantic partners enter adolescents' attachment hierarchies. Methods for assessing adolescents' attachment hierarchies may also lead to new ways of examining individual differences in attachment organization. For instance, individual differences in the developmental timing of forming a peer attachment bond may affect adjustment. On the one hand, adolescents who prematurely replace a parent with a peer as their primary attachment figure may be at risk for externalizing or problem behaviors, while on the other hand, teens who delay transfer of attachment functions to a peer relationship may be at risk for anxiety or depressive symptoms.

The Interplay of Sexual, Affiliative, and Attachment Systems

> It seems certain that another major shift takes place with the onset of adolescence, ushered in by hormonal changes. This development leads the young person to begin a search for a partnership with an age peer, usually of the opposite sex—a relationship in which reproductive and caregiving systems, as well as the attachment system, are involved [Ainsworth, 1989 p. 710].

Although adolescents rely on peers or romantic partners to serve safe haven and secure base functions (Chapter Two, this volume), few of these relationships meet criteria for an enduring attachment bond. Ainsworth characterized an "affectional bond" as "a relatively long enduring tie in which the partner is important as a unique individual and interchangeable with none other" (p. 711). These bonds are characterized by a desire to maintain closeness and distress when the individual is "inexplicably" separated from his or her partner. Attachment relationships meet criteria for an affectional bond but differ from other affectional bonds by providing comfort at times of distress and confidence in the face of challenge. Most children enter adolescence with attachment bonds to parents that can be traced back to infancy. Puberty marks the emergence of reproductive capacity, the activation of the sexual behavior system, and the initiation of a search for a partnership with an age peer. This search typically results in the formation of an attachment bond in which the peer partner becomes a primary attachment figure and shares responsibility for caring for offspring. Although there is considerable variation in when a peer attachment bond is established, the search for such a partnership initiates a fundamental reorganization of adolescents' relationships with parents and peers.

NEW DIRECTIONS FOR CHILD AND ADOLESCENT DEVELOPMENT • DOI: 10.1002/cd

The reorganization of relationships with parents and peers is motivated by a reorganization of behavioral systems that occurs with the onset of puberty. As the sexual system becomes more active, it alters the interplay between the attachment and affiliative systems. In many respects, the sexual system works in synchrony with the affiliative system. The roots of affiliative behavior can be traced to the child's ability to distinguish familiar from unfamiliar individuals (Furman, 1999). Familiar individuals tend to activate proximity and affiliative behavior, and unfamiliar individuals tend to activate the fear system. Whereas during middle childhood, the affiliation system maintains engagement with friends and peer groups, the affiliative system in adolescence supports the emergence of dating and romantic relationships (Connolly et al., 2000; Dunphy, 1963). The synchronous interplay of sexual and affiliative systems increases emotional involvement in peer relationships while reducing time spent with adult caregivers. This increased involvement with friends and romantic partners creates opportunities for developing competencies that contribute to the eventual formation of a peer attachment bond. During adolescence, affiliative and sexual systems tend to take precedence over the attachment system, which contributes to a sense of distancing or disengaging from parents (see Chapter One, this volume).

Increased involvement with friends creates new opportunities to test peers as potential attachment figures. Waters and Cummings (2000) have described ad hoc attachment relationships in which a partner serves a secure base or safe haven function but does not become a primary or secondary attachment figure. The ad hoc nature of these relationships provides teens with opportunities to develop reciprocal interaction skills in emotionally challenging situations. Teens are most likely to rely on peers when parents are not readily accessible, in contexts in which their age-mates are better positioned to provide support or encouragement, and in situations that elicit low-level activation of the attachment system. For instance, problems with teachers and anxiety about romantic rejection may provide opportunities to test peers as ad hoc attachment figures (Waters & Cummings, 2000). Peers may also serve as a secure base for joining group activities, having contact with the opposite sex, or initiating dating relationships. These situations represent relatively low levels of threat or challenge.

The contributions of sexual, affiliative, and attachment systems to peer relationships change over the course of adolescence. Early adolescence is a period in which the activation of the sexual or reproductive system increases teens' emotional involvement in peer relationships. In addition to serving low-level attachment functions, teens' friendships promote increased intimacy and self-disclosure (Collins & Sroufe, 1999). Close friendships provide adolescents with opportunities to seek autonomy from caregivers and experiment with peers for companionship and advice seeking (Collins & Repinski, 1994). This developmental process enables adolescents to further individuate and differentiate from parents (Grotevant & Cooper, 1985). Some of this increased intimacy with peers serves an attachment function.

For instance, as early adolescents increase their time spent with peers, they are likely to rely on peers for support at times of low stress or for encouragement to face challenges. Yet this experimentation with peers as ad hoc attachment figures (Waters & Cummings, 2000) is often transitory and rarely results in the formation of an enduring attachment bond or reliance on peers in dangerous or high-stress situations. Although friend and romantic relationships do not result in the formation of attachment bonds, they do play an important role in teens' developing concepts of self in romantic relationships (Brown, 1999).

By midadolescence, friendships and romantic relationships are perceived as greater sources of intimacy and companionship than relationships with parents (Buhrmester & Furman, 1987; Furman & Wehner, 1997). Friendships facilitate the development of romantic relationships in several ways. First, sharing thoughts and feelings related to romantic attractions may provide the basis for increased intimacy that characterizes close friendships (Furman & Buhrmester, 1992). Second, peer relationships provide a context for both interacting with prospective romantic partners and acquiring social skills required for the development and maintenance of a romantic relationship (Connolly et al., 2000; Dunphy, 1963). Furman (1999) has argued that relationships that are primarily motivated by the affiliative system provide a context in which teens develop the skills required for forming an enduring romantic relationship. More specifically, reciprocity, cooperation, and reciprocal altruism are competencies required for developing and sustaining a romantic relationship. In addition, friendships help teens to develop conflict negotiation skills (Collins & Sroufe, 1999).

By late adolescence, some friendships or romantic relationships have become more enduring attachment bonds (Connolly et al., 2000). Several factors likely contribute to increased activation of the attachment system during late adolescence. First, the search for a partnership with a same-age peer becomes more focused as teens move away from parents and face the prospects of living independently. Second, older adolescents and young adults face the challenges of forming an identity and entering adult roles that may make their need for a secure base more acute. There is some evidence that the experience of loneliness increases as young adults tend to lack regular contact with parents or close relationship with peers (Russell, Cutrona, Rose, & Yurko, 1984). Together these factors are likely to orient teens to the potential security provided by a close friend or romantic relationship. Clues that may indicate a partner's commitment to an enduring relationship are likely to become more salient as teens seek partners with whom they can form an enduring bond.

In summary, while early adolescents begin to use peers for attachment functions, by midadolescence teens may rely on a close friend or romantic partner as a safe haven or secure base in contexts involving relatively low levels of danger or challenge. Not only do these situations allow teens to test peers as ad hoc attachment figures, but they also offer opportunities for teens to provide caregiving support to distressed or challenged friends or romantic partners. In this sense, close friends and dating partners provide a context for experimenting with the skills required for forming adult attachment bonds.

Attachment Bonds with Parents During Adolescence

Attachment bonds with parents form an important background for teens' exploration of peer relationships. These bonds are evident in teens' continuous monitoring of parents' whereabouts and availability. Brief daily contacts, along with more frequent instrumental and financial support, are often enough to maintain adolescents' confidence in their parents' availability. This daily monitoring allows teens' attachment concerns to recede to the background and permits the affiliative and sexual systems to take precedence. As a result, parents' continuing roles as primary attachment figures are likely to be evident only in situations that elicit high levels of attachment system activation. For instance, the attachment system can rapidly take precedence over affiliative and sexual behavioral systems when teens appraise situations as threats to the caregiver's availability (Ainsworth, 1989; Bowlby, 1973), dangerous, or challenging (Bretherton, 1980). Situations involving danger may be quite infrequent but include serious illness, accidents, and assault. Threats to parental availability include family conflict, parental illness, and loss. Finally, in situations involving challenge, the attachment system may be activated at lower levels. Parents are likely to be used as a secure base for situations in which they have instrumental knowledge or expertise, such as learning to drive, getting a job, or making plans for the future (Scharf, Mayseless, & Kivenson-Baron, 2004).

In spite of the persistence of teens' attachment bonds with parents, these relationships undergo dramatic changes as teens develop increased autonomy and self-regulation (see Chapter One, this volume). A number of studies have demonstrated that parent-teen conflict is normative and allows teens to gain jurisdiction over decisions ranging from curfew to school involvement to friendship choice (Laursen & Collins, 1994; Smetana, 1996). The quality of communication between parents and teens during this period is important in renegotiating a cooperative partnership (Allen & Land, 1999; Kobak & Duemmler, 1994). Parental monitoring plays an important role in ensuring that teens successfully manage increased exposure to dangerous situations or opportunities to engage in risky behavior. Teen problem behaviors such as unprotected sexual activity, substance use, and other forms of delinquent activity may jeopardize their safety and often call for parental involvement. When teens are faced with situations involving serious danger or decisions related to reproductive strategies, their attachment systems are more likely to be activated at high levels, leading to a preference for parent or adult attachment figures over peers. As Weiss (1982, 1991) suggested, parents continue to remain primary attachment figures and serve as "attachment figures in reserve."

Developmental Change in Adolescents' Attachment Hierarchies

We have suggested that adolescence can be viewed as a period in which teens begin to form attachment bonds with romantic partners or close friends and reorganize attachment bonds with parents. Hazan and Zeifman (1994) framed this developmental perspective and provided a method for identifying adolescents' primary attachment figures. They proposed a process in which proximity seeking, safe haven, and secure base functions were transferred from parents to a romantic partner or close friend in a sequential fashion. Their WHOTO interview asked participants to whom they would go for different attachment needs. Through these questions, participants identify targets of proximity-seeking behaviors ("Who is the person you most like to spend time with?"), safe haven ("Who would you go to help you feel better when something bad happens to you or you are emotionally upset?"), separation protest ("Who is the person you don't like to be away from?"), and secure base function ("Who do you count on to always be there for you and care about you no matter what?"). Hazan and Zeifman suggested that a romantic partner becomes a primary attachment figure when attachment functions are fully transferred, a process that typically requires a relationship that endures for at least two years.

Since Hazan and Zeifman's pivotal study (1994), a number of researchers have employed versions of the WHOTO interview to determine an individual's primary attachment figure. Two studies investigated college students' attachment relationships. Fraley and Davis (1997) used a revised version of the WHOTO interview with a sample of college students. They asked participants to write the names of people who "best served" proximity seeking, safe haven, and secure base functions. The first name listed in response to each question was used to identify primary attachment figures. Results confirmed Hazan and Zeifman's sequence (1994) in the transfer of attachment functions. Peers (romantic partners or friends) were nominated for proximity seeking and safe haven functions, and parents were somewhat more likely to be identified as serving secure base functions. When a romantic relationship lasted more than two years, students were more likely to identify their romantic partner as serving a secure base function.

Trinke and Bartholomew (1997) used a revised version of the WHOTO scale to measure college students' relationships with multiple attachment figures. Thirty-six percent of the students identified their mothers as primary figures, 31 percent identified romantic partners, 14 percent identified best friends, 11 percent fathers, and 8 percent siblings. Of the students who were in romantic relationships, 62 percent identified their partners as a primary attachment figure, and 30 percent identified their mother or father as primary. For students who were not in a romantic relationship, 64 percent identified their mother or father as primary, and 22 percent identified a best friend as a primary attachment figure.

High school students are less likely than college students to identify a peer as an attachment figure. Freeman and Brown (2001) asked sixteen to eighteen year olds to name the one person they "rely on most for emotional support and closeness." A parent was identified as primary by 47 percent of the respondents, peers or siblings were identified as primary by 43 percent, and the self was identified by 10 percent. Mothers were nominated ten times more frequently than fathers, and romantic partners were nominated more frequently than friends. Teens with higher levels of self-reported attachment security were more likely to nominate parents as primary figures, and insecure teens were more likely to nominate peers as primary figures (Freeman & Brown, 2001).

Studies of children indicate that preadolescents rarely identify peers as serving attachment functions. Nickerson and Nagle (2005) employed Fraley and Davis's revised WHOTO measure (1997) with a sample of fourth, sixth, and eighth graders. Children circled the category of person (parent, grandparent, sibling, best friend, romantic partner, or other) they preferred for each situation. Nominations of peers for proximity and safe haven functions increased between the fourth and eighth grades, but both groups of children identified parents as serving secure base functions (Nickerson & Nagle, 2005). Kerns, Tomich, and Kim (2006) asked third and sixth graders to respond to four attachment situations (times when children felt sad, tired, sick, or scared) and two companionship situations (wanting to play or tell someone a secret). Whereas over 90 percent of third and fifth graders nominated parents in attachment situations, peers were nominated in 74 to 90 percent of companionship situations. Kerns and her colleagues emphasize the importance of considering context in evaluating proximity seeking (Kerns et al., 2006). Even in middle childhood, children seek proximity to peers in contexts involving affiliation or companionship independent of whom they seek out for attachment needs.

Previous studies of children's, adolescents', and young adults' attachment figures generally converge on several important points. First, the use of peers to serve attachment functions increases over the course of adolescence. Second, by late adolescence, many teens identify a romantic partner or friend as a primary attachment figure. Third, romantic partners are preferred over close friends as primary attachment figures in late adolescence. Fourth, romantic relationships that endure are more likely to become attachment relationships. Together, these findings support Ainsworth's claim (1989) that puberty marks the beginning of a search for a partnership with a same age peer.

Although previous studies document a developmental reorganization of attachment relationships, they have several important limitations. The original attachment functions proposed by Hazan and Zeifman (1994), including proximity seeking, separation distress, safe haven, and secure base, have not been systematically assessed or validated. For example, proximity seeking may be motivated by affiliative as well as attachment concerns (Kerns et al., 2006). Second, the distinction between relationships that serve safe haven and secure base functions is not clearly differentiated from relationships that meet criteria for an affectional bond. Ainsworth's criteria

(1989) focus on the enduring nature of the relationship and the separation distress that would ensue from inexplicable separation from an attachment figure. Finally, although previous studies generally support the notion that friends or romantic partners can become primary attachment figures by late adolescence, the exclusive focus on identifying a primary attachment figure minimizes the complexity of teens' ongoing negotiation of multiple relationships with parents, romantic partners, and close friends. As a result, little is known about the role that secondary or tertiary attachment figures play in adolescents' social networks. We believe that adolescent attachments may be better conceived in the context of an individual's hierarchy of attachment relationships. The hierarchy concept captures how individuals maintain multiple attachment bonds, while ordering their preferences for attachment figures at times when their attachment systems are activated.

Adolescent Attachment Hierarchies: Conceptual and Measurement Issues

Bowlby's concept of an attachment hierarchy has been largely ignored by attachment research that has focused on identifying a single primary attachment figure. The notion that individuals can have hierarchically organized preferences for multiple attachment figures provides a way of understanding how peers begin to serve ad hoc attachment functions during adolescence without becoming attachment figures. The major adaptive advantage of an attachment hierarchy is that it provides the child, adolescent, or adult with alternative caregivers if a primary caregiver is unavailable. Adolescents' attachment hierarchies can be understood in terms of their preferences for particular people at times when their attachment system is activated. These preferences will guide teens' choice of attachment figures during times of danger (safe haven) and times of challenge (secure base).

The attachment hierarchy is an organized set of preferences for persons whom the individual seeks out when the attachment system is activated (Colin, 1996). In her classic study of infants in Uganda, Ainsworth observed that while infants displayed attachment behaviors toward multiple caregivers, they also showed clear preferences for particular caregivers across a range of situations, including when the caregiver left the infant or when the infant was alarmed, tired, hungry, or ill (Ainsworth, 1967). Cummings (1980) used a laboratory procedure to assess infants' preferences for mothers and day care providers and found that children showed clear preferences for mothers. A similar laboratory procedure was used to assess infant preferences for mothers and fathers (Colin, 1996). In support of the hierarchy construct, Colin observed that 70 percent of her sample showed clear preferences for their mother over their father during moments of attachment system activation. Infants who did show a preference for their fathers had fathers who spent more time with them and took on more caregiving responsibilities.

NEW DIRECTIONS FOR CHILD AND ADOLESCENT DEVELOPMENT • DOI: 10.1002/cd

These studies suggest two general principles that should guide assessment of an individual's preferences for attachment figures. First, preferences must be observed during situations in which the attachment system is activated. As children mature, the attachment system is activated less frequently. As a result, a growing number of social interactions are motivated by sexual, affiliative, or exploratory behavioral systems that do not involve the attachment system or preferences for attachment figures (Ainsworth, 1991). The growing complexity of teens' social relationships makes it important for researchers to distinguish situations that activate the attachment system from situations in which other motivational systems are active (Goldberg, Grusec, & Jenkins, 1999). Three general types of appraisals can activate the attachment system in infants, older children, and adults: appraisals of threat to the attachment figure's availability (Bowlby, 1973; Ainsworth, 1989; Kobak, 1999), appraisals of danger or distress that lead the individual to use the caregiver as a safe haven (Bretherton, 1980), or appraisals of challenge that lead the individual to use the caregiver as a secure base (Waters & Cummings, 2000). In addition, attachment figures are expected to demonstrate consistent availability across time and place or to demonstrate commitment (Duemmler & Kobak, 2001) or investment in maintaining the relationship (Howes, 1999). These expectations mark attachment figures as among the most important people in the child's life.

A second principle for assessing the attachment hierarchy requires observing the child's preferences in situations where multiple caregivers are equally accessible. Main (1999) suggests several laboratory paradigms for assessing young children's preferences for two attachment figures. These laboratory settings are designed to provide the child with equal access to two caregivers. However, naturally occurring situations rarely meet this equal access criterion. Although attachment behaviors can be observed in naturally occurring contexts of danger, challenge, or threat to the caregivers' availability, the child's options for seeking support from multiple caregivers are usually constrained by the caregivers' physical proximity. As children grow older, they face a growing number of challenges and threats in settings in which only peers and nonparental adults are immediately accessible. These peers and adults may serve attachment functions without actually meeting criteria for serving as attachment figures (Waters & Cummings, 2000), thus complicating the use of observations for assessing adolescents' preference for different attachment figures.

Interviews offer a valuable solution to the challenge of assessing teens' preferences for attachment figures. The Important People Interview was developed to assess attachment preferences in older children (Kobak, Rosenthal, & Serwik, 2004). This interview approach offers several advantages over behavioral observations and previous interview techniques. First, open-ended nominations allow the individual to identify the important people in his or her life. This differs from the categorical approach that preemptively identifies potential attachment figures by categories such as mother, father, sibling, or day care provider. Second, preferences can be assessed in response to hypothetical situations generated by the interviewer. Hypothetical situations make it possible to generate contexts that would activate the attachment system while structuring equal access to multiple attachment figures. Finally, by asking the individual to rank multiple caregivers, interview methodology allows subjects to clarify their preferences for different caregivers. In sum, an interview assessment can provide both normative and individual difference information on how children, adolescents, and adults organize their attachment relationships.

By assessing the extent to which teens have organized preferences for attachment figures, interview methods may provide a better portrait of change in attachment relationships with parents and peers. For instance, peers may be nominated as serving attachment functions after parents and thus may enter a teen's attachment hierarchy as a tertiary or secondary figure. If a peer relationship endures or occurs in a context in which the teen is living in closer proximity to the peer than to the parent, the peer may move to a primary place in the attachment hierarchy. However, a parent who previously occupied a primary place in the hierarchy would likely move into a secondary position. This secondary position is consistent with what Weiss (1982) described as parents' acting as an attachment figure in reserve during late adolescence and early adulthood. This position can provide teens with an important backup if the primary peer attachment relationship becomes distressed or dissolves.

Our review of previous studies suggests that the situations used to identify attachment figures should focus on characteristics of the attachment bond identified by Ainsworth (1989). These include the enduring nature of the relationship (someone the adolescent can "always count on"), separation distress (whom the adolescent would miss the most), a feeling of closeness (whom the adolescent feels closest to), or secure base or safe haven (whom the adolescent would seek in times of high stress or danger). By focusing on these aspects, researchers can more clearly differentiate between relationships that may serve attachment functions and relationships that meet criteria for enduring attachment bonds.

Reorganization of Attachment Hierarchies During Adolescence

Reorganization of the attachment hierarchy is a gradual process during which a peer may enter the attachment hierarchy and over time replace a parent as a primary attachment figure. Although studies of American and Canadian middle-class populations suggest that this reorganization typically plays out over the course of adolescence, there is substantial variability in when the process of reorganization begins and how quickly it proceeds. Deviations from the typical timing of reorganization may occur in the form of premature reorganization in which a peer becomes a primary attachment figure by early or midadolescence or in the form of delayed reorganization in which a parent remains a primary attachment figure well into adulthood.

NEW DIRECTIONS FOR CHILD AND ADOLESCENT DEVELOPMENT • DOI: 10.1002/cd

Premature reorganization of teens' attachment hierarchies can be identified during early and midadolescence. It is likely to be evident when primary or secondary positions in teens' attachment hierarchies are occupied by friends, siblings, or romantic partners rather than by parents or adult caregivers. This pattern of premature reorganization may represent a risk factor for several types of adjustment difficulties, including association with deviant peers, sexual risk-taking behaviors, and susceptibility to peer pressure to engage in delinquent or antisocial behavior (Goldstein, Davis-Kean, & Eccles, 2005). Dishion has described this developmental dynamic as one in which teens gain "premature autonomy" from parents (Dishion, Nelson, & Bullock, 2004).

The quality of relationships with parents and peers may play an important role in predisposing teens to premature reorganization of their attachment hierarchies. Attachment theory suggests that although children seek protection and support from parents, not all parents are available and responsive to their children's attachment needs. During late childhood and early adolescence, parental availability and responsiveness includes monitoring activities with peers and school and respecting the growing need for autonomy and self-regulation. When parents successfully respond to these needs, children are likely to feel secure and confident in their parents' availability. Thus, parents' warmth and involvement can protect teens from premature reliance on peers and subsequent problem behavior (Vitaro, Brendgen, & Tremblay, 2000). In contrast, lack of parental availability and anxious attachment increase the likelihood that teens will turn prematurely to peers for attachment-related needs. Lack of caregiver monitoring and discipline has been associated with teens' affiliating with deviant peers and subsequent delinquency (Galambos, Barker, & Almeida, 2003; Gutman & Eccles, 1999).

Peer factors may also contribute to premature reorganization of the attachment hierarchy. Affiliation with deviant peers has been identified as a risk factor for adolescent antisocial behavior. These peer affiliations support the development and maintenance of aggressive, delinquent, and problem behaviors over the course of adolescence (Patterson, Dishion, & Yoerger, 2000). Different hypotheses about teens' motivation for affiliating with deviant peers have been posited. Children with histories of aggressive behavior tend to affiliate with peers who share their aggressive tendencies. Several processes evident in deviant peer groups may increase teens' attempts at forming a peer attachment bond. The attempt to emulate more "mature" behaviors and increased likelihood of sexual involvement may result in increased emotional engagement in a dating relationship. In addition, the general alienation from adult values and increased susceptibility to peer pressure that characterizes deviant peer groups may move teens toward disengagement from parents and premature reliance on peers. Although these factors may incline teens toward viewing their relationship with a peer as a bond, relationships formed in this context are less likely to have the stability or enduring quality that characterizes a committed adult pair-bond.

Ecological or sociocultural factors may also contribute to premature reorganization of teens' attachment hierarchies. For instance, tracking of students by achievement levels in middle school increases the likelihood that low-achieving students will be grouped together (Dodge & Pettit, 2003). Poor achievement may promote school disengagement, which in turn increases the likelihood that teens will focus on peer relationships and short-term peer status or enhanced maturity that they may perceive as resulting from early sexual relationships. In addition, minority racial status increases the likelihood of deviant peer affiliation and affiliation with deviant peers (McCabe, Hough, Wood, & Yeh, 2001). Poverty may also be associated with reproductive strategies that favor earlier childbearing and place less emphasis on the formation of adult pair-bonds. Although teen pregnancy in Western industrial societies is often associated with a range of adjustment problems, earlier transfer of attachment function may be quite adaptive in cultures characterized by high levels of resource scarcity. These sociocultural factors create different expectations for the transfer of attachment function.

The timing of puberty is an additional factor that may increase the likelihood of premature reorganization of teens' attachment hierarchies. There is substantial variability in the timing of puberty in both girls and boys. Early puberty, particularly among girls, has been associated with a variety of adjustment difficulties, including teen pregnancy, depression, anxiety, aggression, and substance abuse (Ellis, 2004). The activation of the sexual behavioral system is likely to accelerate peer and romantic involvement, which may increase transfer of attachment functions from parents to peers. Children experiencing early puberty may have difficulty relating to same-age peers and thus move toward affiliation with older peers, often without the self-regulatory capacities that develop during early adolescence. While early puberty is a risk factor for adjustment difficulties, parental involvement and maintenance of parents as primary attachment figures may serve a protective function for early-maturing teens.

While some teens prematurely place peers in their attachment hierarchies, others may inappropriately delay their entry. Delayed reorganization of teens' attachment hierarchies may be evident in several ways. First, assessments that systematically assess secondary and perhaps tertiary figures can establish norms for when peers enter teens' attachment hierarchies. Based on such norms, teens who do not show preference for a peer attachment figure when their age-mates do (typically mid- to late adolescence) might be considered delayed in reorganizing their attachment hierarchy. Second, another type of delay could be evident among teens who rely on adults rather than peers for affiliative functions of enjoyable companionship and activities. Teens who are socially isolated from peer relationships may lack the competencies and contextual support provided by peers for forming an enduring peer attachment bond.

Adolescents who delay reorganization of their attachment hierarchies may face several adjustment difficulties. Continued reliance on parents as primary attachment figures may create tension and conflict in the parent-child relationship. For example, teen mothers who lack romantic partners must often continue to rely on their parents as sources of protection and support. Furthermore, peers who serve as secondary or primary figures often provide support for the transition into adult work roles and greater financial independence from parents. The lack of such relationships may increase the likelihood of continued dependence on parents. Finally, delayed reorganization may be implicated in the development of internalizing symptoms, such as anxiety and depression. These symptoms may make engagement in peer relationships less likely and less rewarding for teens. If left untreated, the pattern of delayed transfer and feelings of depression or anxiety may create a cyclical dynamic that interferes with teen and young adult development.

Summary and Future Directions

The search for an enduring relationship with a peer provides a clear description of the attachment-related task of adolescence. We have argued that this process must be understood as one in which teens must maintain attachments with parents while developing new attachment bonds with peers. Furthermore, this process is best understood as a reorganization of teens' hierarchies of relationships with multiple attachment figures rather than as one in which peers replace parents as primary figures. Measurement of attachment hierarchies requires differentiating between relationships that serve attachment functions and relationships that become enduring attachment bonds. The focus on attachment bonds requires that researchers shift from criteria of proximity maintenance, safe haven, and secure base functions to criteria that are specific to enduring attachment bonds (rankings of closeness, separation distress, and response to danger). Methods for assessing teens' attachment hierarchies will make it possible to consider stability and change in attachment bonds with parents and peers over the course of adolescence. By clearly identifying normative trends in how teens reorganize their attachment hierarchies, we can address new questions about deviations from normative trends and how the quality of attachment bonds with parents influences the transfer of attachment functions from parents to peers.

References

Ainsworth, M.D.S. (1967). *Infancy in Uganda.* Baltimore, MD: Johns Hopkins University Press.

Ainsworth, M.D.S. (1989). Attachment bonds beyond infancy. *American Psychologist, 44,* 709–716.

Ainsworth, M.D.S. (1991). Attachments and other affectional bonds across the life cycle. In C. M. Parkes, J. Stevenson-Hinde, & P. Marris (Eds.), *Attachment across the life cycle* (pp. 33–51). London: Routledge.

Allen, J. P., & Land, D. (1999). Attachment in adolescence. In J. Cassidy & P. Shaver (Eds.), *Handbook of attachment: Theory, research, and clinical implications* (pp. 319–335). New York: Guilford Press.

Bowlby, J. (1969/1982). *Attachment and loss: Vol. 1.* New York: Basic Books.

Bowlby, J. (1973). *Attachment and loss: Anxiety and anger: Vol. 2.* New York: Basic Books.

Bretherton, I. (1980). Young children in stressful situations: The supporting role of attachment figures and unfamiliar caregivers. In G. V. Coelho & P. I. Ahmed (Eds.), *Uprooting and development* (pp. 179–210). New York: Plenum Press.

Brown, B. (1999). "You're going out with who?" Peer group influences on adolescent romantic relationships. In W. Furman, B. B. Brown, & C. Feiring (Eds.), *The development of romantic relationships in adolescence* (pp. 125–147). Cambridge: Cambridge University Press.

Buhrmester, D., & Furman, W. (1987). The development of companionship and intimacy. *Child Development, 58*(4), 1101–1113.

Colin, V. (1996). *Human attachment.* New York: McGraw-Hill.

Collins, W. A., & Repinski, D. J. (1994). Relationships during adolescence: Continuity and change in interpersonal perspective. In R. Montemayor, G. R. Adams, & T. Gullotta (Eds.), *Personal relationships during adolescence* (Vol. 6, pp. 7–36). Thousand Oaks, CA: Sage.

Collins, W. A., & Sroufe, L. A. (1999). Capacity for intimate relationships: A developmental construction. In W. Furman, B. B. Brown, & C. Feiring (Eds.), *The development of romantic relationships in adolescence* (pp. 125–147). Cambridge: Cambridge University Press.

Connolly, J., Furman, W., & Konarski, R. (2000). The role of peers in the emergence of heterosexual romantic relationships in adolescence. *Child Development, 71*(5), 1395–1408.

Cummings, E. M. (1980). Caregiver stability and attachment in infant day care. *Developmental Psychology, 16,* 31–37.

Dishion, T. J., Nelson, S. E., & Bullock, B. M. (2004). Premature adolescent autonomy: Parent disengagement and deviant peer process in the amplification of problem behaviour. *Journal of Adolescence, 27*(5), 515–530.

Dodge, K. A., & Pettit, G. S. (2003). A biopsychosocial model of the development of chronic conduct problems in adolescence. *Developmental Psychology, 39*(2), 349–371.

Doherty, N. A., & Feeney, J. A. (2004). The composition of attachment networks throughout the adult years. *Personal Relationships, 11,* 469–488.

Duemmler, S., & Kobak, R. (2001). The development of attachment and commitment in dating relationships: Attachment security as a relationship construct. *Journal of Adolescence, 24,* 401–415.

Dunphy, D. (1963). The social structure of urban adolescent peer groups. *Sociometry, 26,* 230–246.

Ellis, B. J. (2004). Timing of pubertal maturation in girls: An integrated life history approach. *Psychological Bulletin, 130*(6), 920–958.

Fraley, C., and Davis, K. E. (1997). Attachment formation and transfer in young adults' close friendships and romantic relationships. *Personal Relationships, 4,* 131–144.

Freeman, H., & Brown, B. B. (2001). Primary attachment to parents and peers during adolescence: Differences by attachment style. *Journal of Youth and Adolescence, 30,* 653–674.

Furman, W. (1999). Friends and lovers: The role of peer relationships in adolescent romantic relationships. In W. A. Collins & B. Laursen (Eds.), *Relationships as developmental contexts* (Vol. 30, pp. 133–154). Mahwah, NJ: Erlbaum.

Furman, W., & Buhrmester, D. (1992). Age and sex differences in perceptions of networks of personal relationships. *Child Development, 63*(1), 103–115.

Furman, W., & Wehner, E. A. (1997). Adolescent romantic relationships: A developmental perspective. In S. Shulman & W. A. Collins (Eds.), *Adolescent romantic relationships* (pp. 21–36). San Francisco: Jossey-Bass.

Galambos, N. L., Barker, E. T., & Almeida, D. M. (2003). Parents do matter: Trajectories of change in externalizing and internalizing problems in early adolescence. *Child Development, 74*(2), 578–594.

Goldberg, S., Grusec, J. E., & Jenkins, J. M. (1999). Confidence in protection: Arguments for a narrow definition of attachment. *Journal of Family Psychology, 13,* 475–483.

Goldstein, S. E., Davis-Kean, P. E., & Eccles, J. S. (2005). Parents, peers, and problem behavior: A longitudinal investigation of the impact of relationship perceptions and characteristics on the development of adolescent problem behavior. *Developmental Psychology, 41*(2), 401–413.

Grotevant, H., & Cooper, C. (1985). Patterns of interaction in family relationships: A perspective on individual differences in the development of identity and role-taking skill in adolescence. *Child Development, 29,* 82–100.

Gutman, L. M., & Eccles, J. S. (1999). Financial strain, parenting behaviors, and adolescents' achievement: Testing model equivalence between African American and European American single- and two-parent families. *Child Development, 70*(6), 1464–1476.

Hazan, C., & Zeifman, D. (1994). Sex and the psychological tether. In K. Bartholomew & D. Perlman (Eds.), *Advances in personal relationships: Vol. 5. Attachment processes in adulthood* (pp. 151–178). London: Jessica Kingsley.

Howes, C. (1999). Attachment relationships in the context of multiple caregivers. In J. Cassidy & P. Shaver (Eds.), *Handbook of attachment: Theory, research and clinical applications* (pp. 671–687). New York: Guilford Press.

Kerns, K. A., Tomich, P. L., & Kim, P. (2006). Normative trends in children's perceptions of availability and utilization of attachment figures in middle childhood. *Social Development, 15,* 1–22.

Kobak, R. (1999). The emotional dynamics of attachment relationships: Implications for theory, research and clinical intervention. In J. Cassidy & P. Shaver (Eds.), *Handbook of attachment: Theory, research, and clinical applications* (pp. 21–43). New York: Guilford Press.

Kobak, R., & Duemmler, S. (1994). Attachment and conversation: Toward a discourse analysis of adolescent and adult security. In K. Bartholomew & D. Perlman (Eds.), *Attachment processes in adulthood* (Vol. 5, pp. 121–149). London: Jessica Kingsley.

Kobak, R., Rosenthal, N., & Serwik, A. (2004). The attachment hierarchy in middle childhood: Conceptual and methodological issues. In K. A. Kerns (Ed.), *Attachment in middle childhood* (pp. 71–88). New York: Guilford Press.

Laursen, B., & Collins, W. A. (1994). Interpersonal conflict during adolescence. *Psychological Bulletin, 115,* 197–209.

Main, M. (1999). Epilogue: Attachment theory: Eighteen points with suggestions for future studies. In J. Cassidy & P. Shaver (Eds.), *Handbook of attachment: Theory, research and clinical applications* (pp. 845–887). New York: Guilford Press.

McCabe, K. M., Hough, R., Wood, P. A., & Yeh, M. (2001). Childhood and adolescent onset conduct disorder: A test of the developmental taxonomy. *Journal of Abnormal Child Psychology, 29*(4), 305–316.

Nickerson, A. B., & Nagle, R. J. (2005). Parent and peer attachment in late childhood and early adolescence. *Journal of Early Adolescence, 25,* 223–249.

Patterson, G. R., Dishion, T. J., & Yoerger, K. (2000). Adolescent growth in new forms of problem behavior: Macro- and micro-peer dynamics. *Prevention Science, 1*(1), 3–13.

Russell, D., Cutrona, C. E., Rose, J., & Yurko, K. (1984). Social and emotional loneliness: An examination of Weiss's typology of loneliness. *Journal of Personality and Social Psychology, 46,* 1313–1321.

Scharf, M., Mayseless, O., & Kivenson-Baron, I. (2004). Adolescents' attachment representations and developmental tasks in emerging adulthood. *Developmental Psychology, 40*(3), 430–444.

Smetana, J. G. (1996). Adolescent-parent conflict: Implications for adaptive and maladaptive development. In D. Cicchetti & S. Toth (Eds.), *Adolescence: Opportunities and challenges* (Vol. 7, pp. 1–46). Rochester, NY: University of Rochester Press.

Trinke, S. J., & Bartholomew, K. (1997). Hierarchies of attachment relationships in young adulthood. *Journal of Social and Personal Relationships, 14*, 603–625.

Vitaro, F., Brendgen, M., & Tremblay, R. E. (2000). Influence of deviant friends on delinquency: Searching for moderator variables. *Journal of Abnormal Child Psychology, 28*(4), 313–325.

Waters, E., & Cummings, E. M. (2000). A secure base from which to explore close relationships. *Child Development, 71*(1), 164–172.

Weiss, R. S. (1982). Attachment in adult life. In C. M. Parkes & J. Stevenson-Hinde (Eds.), *The place of attachment in human behavior* (pp. 171–184). New York: Basic Books.

Weiss, R. S. (1991). The attachment bond in childhood and adulthood. In C. M. Parkes, J. Stevenson-Hinde, & P. Marris (Eds.), *Attachment across the life cycle* (pp. 66–76). New York: Tavistock/Routledge.

ROGER KOBAK *is an associate professor in clinical psychology at the University of Delaware.*

NATALIE L. ROSENTHAL *is a graduate student in clinical psychology at the University of Delaware.*

KRISTYN ZAJAC *is a graduate student in clinical psychology at the University of Delaware.*

STEPHANIE D. MADSEN *is an associate professor of psychology at McDaniel College, Westminster, Maryland.*

NEW DIRECTIONS FOR CHILD AND ADOLESCENT DEVELOPMENT • DOI: 10.1002/cd

This chapter examines the theoretically important but understudied question of concordance in adolescent siblings' representations of attachment to parents.

Representations of Attachment to Parents in Adolescent Sibling Pairs: Concordant or Discordant?

Lisa Kiang, Wyndol Furman

The vast majority of adolescents have at least one sibling, and most are raised by the same parent or parents. What then might we expect two adolescent siblings' representations of attachment to parents to be like? Are both siblings likely to exhibit similarly secure or insecure representations, or is it just as likely that one sibling would have a secure representation and the other an insecure one? Surprisingly, we know very little about whether adolescent siblings raised in the same family exhibit concordant representations of attachments to parents, yet we believe the answer to this question has important implications for attachment theory.

The purpose of this chapter is to discuss this issue of sibling concordance during adolescence and its implications for attachment theory. We first present a simple conceptual model that will lead us to expect adolescent siblings' representations of attachment to parents to be relatively concordant. Our model examines theoretical pathways that begin in infancy as well those that are specific to adolescence, because these developmental trajectories that are initiated early on serve as one of the bases for the levels of

Preparation of this manuscript was supported by grant 50106 from the National Institute of Mental Health (W. Furman, PI), grant HD049080 from the National Institute of Child Health and Human Development (W. Furman, PI), and a NIMH Family Research Consortium IV Postdoctoral Fellowship to L. Kiang while at UCLA.

concordance that we would expect in adolescence. We then review the existing but limited empirical research on this topic, which has tended to focus on infants and young children. Next, we describe our own empirical work examining concordance in adolescent sibling pairs. As will be seen, the degree of concordance in either childhood or adolescence is modest at best, which raises some significant questions regarding the accuracy or adequacy of the simple conceptual model. Accordingly, we reexamine the initial concordance model and discuss potential explanations for the modest degree of adolescent siblings' similarity. We discuss the implications for attachment theory and point out important directions for future research.

A Simple Model of Concordance in Adolescents' Representations of Attachment to Parents

Figure 5.1 depicts a simple model of some of the central processes that may determine adolescent siblings' representations of attachment to their parents. Such processes are set into motion early in development and begin with the caregiver. According to attachment theory, a caregiver's own representation of attachment is a primary determinant of his or her caregiving behavior (Bowlby, 1973; Main, Kaplan, & Cassidy, 1985). This process is illustrated by the paths labeled A in Figure 5.1. Consistent with this idea, extensive empirical work has shown that parents with secure attachment representations exhibit warmer and more sensitive parenting behaviors compared to parents with insecure representations (see van IJzendoorn, 1995). Moreover, theory and research suggest that parental representations are generally stable across adulthood (Ammaniti, Speranza, & Candelori, 1996; Crowell, Treboux, & Waters, 2002), thus predicting a caregiving environment for children that remains generally stable through adolescence. If parental caregiving behaviors are driven by parents' stable representations of attachment, then we would theoretically expect siblings who are raised in the same family to experience similar caregiving behaviors. Of course, mothers and fathers have unique and potentially different representations and may provide different caregiving, but each should provide similar caregiving to their different children.

Ultimately, children's caregiving experiences are expected to shape the quality of their attachment relationships with their parents (paths B in Figure 5.1). Dating back to early observational and laboratory work by Ainsworth, Blehar, Waters, and Wall (1978), research has demonstrated links between parents' caregiving and children's later attachment relationships. As described by Ainsworth and colleagues (1978), a child with a secure attachment relationship has typically experienced a history of sensitive and responsive experiences with his or her caregiver. An inconsistent history of caregiving results in an insecure/ambivalent pattern of attachment. Rejecting and unresponsive experiences are linked to an insecure/avoidant attachment relationship. The idea that children's caregiving experiences play an important role in their subsequent attachment relationship

Figure 5.1. Simple Conceptual Model of Sibling Attachment Concordance

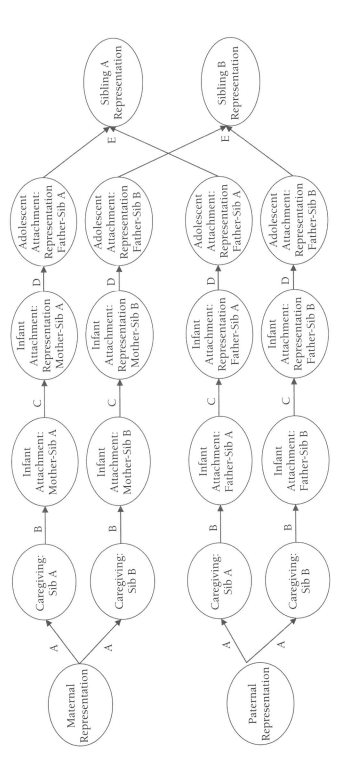

has been consistently supported in the field. For instance, in a meta-analysis of over sixty studies, De Wolff and van IJzendoorn (1997) reported that maternal sensitivity was significantly associated with the security of infants' attachment relationships, providing empirical evidence for paths B.

If a parent's representation is predictive of caregiving (paths A) and such caregiving is predictive of infant attachment (paths B), parental representations should be predictive of insecurity. In a meta-analysis of eighteen studies, van IJzendoorn (1995) reported large effect sizes between parents' representations and infant attachment. Coupling this finding with the evidence that a parent's representation of attachment is stable, we would expect that two siblings would have similar attachments to a particular parent.

Children's attachment-relevant experiences with a parent lead to the development of representations (working models) of their attachment to each parent (paths C) (Main et al., 1985). If they have had similar attachment-relevant experiences with a parent, the two infant siblings should develop similar representations.

Thus far, we have focused our theoretical discussion on infants and children, as the processes that occur then serve as a bases for attachment in adolescence. Throughout childhood, attachment representations are expected to be relatively stable (paths D) (Bowlby, 1980). Thus, if two infant siblings had similar representations of their relationships with a parent, we would expect these siblings to remain relatively similar over time, even into adolescence. Representations of relationships would be expected to change if there were actual changes in each sibling's caregiving experience (Main et al., 1985). However, given that adolescents' representations of attachment to their parents are determined by their attachment-relevant experiences with each parent (paths B), which are determined by each parent's stable representation of attachment (paths A), such changes in adolescents' experiences would not be expected usually, and, hence, changes in their attachment representations from childhood to adolescence would not be expected either.

With the onset of formal operations, adolescents begin to think about representations themselves; that is, they can step out of their specific attachment relationships and think about how it functions (Main et al., 1985). They may be able to develop some perspective on why they and their parents act the way they do and change how they think about the relationship or attachment more generally. Moreover, as a result of such reflections, their separate representations of attachment with different caregivers tend to coalesce into a single representation of attachment to their parents (paths E) (Bretherton, 1985; Main, 1999; Main & Goldwyn, 1984). Consistent with this idea, adolescents' representations of their attachment relationships with mothers and fathers are related to each other (Furman & Simon, 2004). Thus, if two siblings entered adolescence with similar representations of their relationships with their mother and similar representations of their father, one might expect that their coalesced representations would be similar unless the two siblings had substantially different reflections about their relationships.

Our simple model thus suggests an intergenerational cycle wherein parents' representations of attachment affect their caregiving (paths A), which then affects the parent-child attachment relationship (paths B), and thus children's representations of their attachments to parents (paths C). Such representations are expected to be relatively stable (paths D) and, during adolescence, coalesce into a generalized representation of attachment to parents (paths E). As this process begins with each parent's own representation of attachment (paths A), which should have a similar impact on their different children, this model would lead us to expect concordance in adolescents siblings' representations of their attachments to parents.

Research on Sibling Attachment Concordance

Given such a basic and fundamentally important question regarding siblings' attachment concordance, there has been remarkably little empirical work in the area. What little research does exist has focused on children and has generally found a weak to moderate concordance. To provide a common metric for comparing studies, we calculated kappas from tables presented in other work. In one of the first studies examining sibling attachment concordance in infants, Ward, Vaughn, and Robb (1988) found that siblings exhibited significant but modest concordance in the security versus insecurity of their attachment relationships, as measured by the Strange Situation at twelve months ($\kappa = .18$ along a secure-insecure dimension; $\kappa = .23$ along a three-category classification). More recently, van IJzendoorn et al. (2000) incorporated sibling data from three international research groups. Using Strange Situation data across 138 sibling pairs, they found a modest concordance in security versus insecurity ($\kappa = .23$). Notably, rates of concordance were significant only when infant attachments were classified as secure or insecure (versus more specific attachment classifications).

In a twin study, O'Connor and Croft (2001) examined 110 preschool-aged sibling twin pairs and found modest concordance in attachment as measured using a four-category classification from the Strange Situation. Moreover, rates of concordance were similar across monozygotic ($\kappa = .25$ along a four-category classification; $\kappa = .40$ along a secure-insecure dimension) and dizygotic ($\kappa = .21$ and $\kappa = .28$ along a four-category and two-category classification, respectively) sibling twins, supporting the idea that environmental factors such as parental representations and caregiving behavior are significant primary contributors to the development of secure representations. Similarly, Bokhorst et al. (2003) found modest concordance in a sample of 157 twins ($\kappa = .18$ along both a four-category and secure-insecure classification); concordance was slightly higher in dizygotic twins than monozygotic twins ($\kappa = .22$ versus .12 along both a four-category and secure-insecure classification).

The scant existing data suggest a modest concordance in siblings' attachment in childhood. As yet, we do not know how concordant adolescents' representations of attachments to parents are. Adolescence, however, is a particularly interesting period of development during which to examine sibling attachment concordance. Adolescents will have had years of experience with their parents to form representations of these relationships; moreover, these relationships undergo significant changes during this period as adolescents develop autonomy and prepare to leave home. Relatedly, the process of transferring attachment figures from a parent to a romantic partner typically begins in adolescence (Furman & Wehner, 1994; Hazan & Zeifman, 1994). Finally, independent representations of attachments to parents are hypothesized to coalesce into a single state of mind during this time, as depicted by paths E in our model (see Chapter Three, this volume). As adolescents acquire the cognitive skills and sophistication of formal operations, they are able to step back and reflect on their relationships. Such metacognition leads to an integration of previous attachment experiences into a more generalized representation of attachment to parents (Bretherton, 1985; Main, 1999; Main & Goldwyn, 1984). Taken together, it is clearly important to examine adolescents' representations of their attachment relationships and the concordance in siblings' representations.

An Empirical Study of Adolescent Siblings' Concordance in Representations

We examined the degree of concordance in adolescent siblings' representations of their attachment relationships with parents. Data consisted of forty-one sibling pairs, drawn from a subset of a larger study on adolescent social relationships. Adolescents who were originally targeted for recruitment were in the twelfth grade (M age = 17.85 years, SD = .46). One of the target adolescent's siblings was then recruited for this particular project. Siblings' age ranged from 15.10 to 22.99 years (M age = 17.53 years, SD = 2.20). The ethnic diversity of the sample resembled general proportions found in the United States: 63 percent European American, 12 percent Latin American, 9 percent African American, and 4 percent Asian American.

Adolescents' representations of attachment to parents were assessed using the Adult Attachment Interview (AAI; George, Kaplan, & Main, 1985). Interviews were administered and tape-recorded by trained interviewers, transcribed, and then coded by individuals certified in the AAI coding system. Approximately 20 percent of the interviews in the larger study were double-coded ($n = 21$); interrater agreement of the classifications was satisfactory ($\kappa = .84$). Interrater agreement on the loving scores and coherence of transcript scores was also satisfactory (ICC = .73 to .86).

First, we examined the adolescent siblings' concordance across four attachment classification categories. As shown in Table 5.1, we found little evidence of concordance ($\kappa = .11$). We found similarly low levels of concordance when classifications were collapsed into secure versus insecure categories ($\kappa = .08$).

Table 5.1. Cross-Tabulation of Siblings' Attachment Classifications

	Sibling 1				
	Secure	Dismissing	Preoccupied	Unresolved	Total N
Sibling 2					
Secure	24% (10)	17% (7)	0% (0)	5% (2)	19
Dismissing	20% (8)	25% (10)	0% (0)	2% (1)	19
Preoccupied	2% (1)	0% (0)	0% (0)	0% (0)	1
Unresolved	2% (1)	0% (0)	2% (1)	0% (0)	2
Total N	20	17	1	3	41

$N = 41$, $\kappa = .11$; $p = .37$.

To shed further light on our findings, we explored several family variables that could potentially moderate rates of concordance. For instance, it is possible that concordance is greater in same-gender dyads, as one might expect the caregiving of two siblings of the same gender to be more similar than the caregiving of two siblings of the different gender. We had twenty-four same-gender dyads and seventeen mixed-gender dyads but found the degree of concordance to be similar across gender configurations ($\kappa = .08$ and .15, respectively). Thus, siblings' gender did not appear to play an explanatory role in rates of attachment concordance. If anything, siblings in mixed-gender dyads exhibit slightly higher rates of concordance. Second, it is possible that concordance would be greater if siblings were closer in age, as they may be more likely to have similar caregiving experiences. We divided the sample into those who were two years or less apart ($n = 24$) and those with an age spacing that was wider than two years ($n = 17$). Levels of concordance were again similar and slightly biased against expectations ($\kappa = .07$ and .16, respectively). Third, it is possible that concordance for a twelfth-grade adolescent and a younger sibling would be greater because both siblings are living at home. Although the finding was nonsignificant, there was a slight trend in that direction ($\kappa = .19$ in the twenty-five pairs in which the sibling was younger; .08 in the sixteen pairs in which the sibling was older). Fourth, we examined whether concordance varied as a function of whether the two were closer to the same parent or to different parents. When both said they were closer to the same parent or both said they were equally close to both parents ($n = 26$), a moderate level of concordance was found ($\kappa = .31$, $p = .06$). When one said he or she was closer to one parent and the other said he or she was not closer to that parent (either because he or she was closer to the other parent or equally close to both parents; $n = .14$), the concordance was negative though nonsignificant ($\kappa = -.20$). This potential difference is discussed subsequently.

Finally, we examined the degree of similarity in two of the more comprehensive scales on the AAI—loving behavior and coherence of transcript.

The loving scales are a comprehensive rating of the loving and unloving behavior of each parent, whereas the coherence scale is the most comprehensive index of the quality of the discourse. Interestingly, the two siblings' ratings of loving behavior by each parent were significantly related: mother ($r = .52$, $p < .01$) and father ($r = .29$, $p < .05$). Like the classification scores, the two siblings' coherence of transcript were not significantly related, $r = .07$. The greater concordance in experiences compared to representations is noteworthy because the attachment-related scales and classifications are derived from the same interview, which would make the correlations more likely to be similar than if independent measures had been used. This difference between concordance in representations and experience is discussed subsequently.

A Reexamination of a Simple Model of Sibling Concordance

Although each path in the conceptual model is generally supported by both theoretical and empirical work, prior research with infant siblings and analyses using our own data with adolescent sibling pairs suggest that the degree of sibling concordance is modest at best. These findings indicate that a reexamination of the specific paths in the model is warranted.

According to paths A and B in our conceptual model, parental representations influence caregiving sensitivity, which in turn affects infants' attachment relationships with caregivers. Analyses of multiple studies reveal that the link between parental representations and infant's attachment is relatively large (for example, $\kappa = .49$; van IJzendoorn, 1995). Putting together our model and this empirical information, we can use basic computational procedures of path analysis to estimate the expected covariation between two siblings' attachment (Loehlin, 2004). Specifically, the covariation between two siblings' attachment would be expected to be equal to the product of the links between parental representation and the attachment of the two siblings. Thus, we would expect the covariation to be approximately .24 (.49 $\times$ .49). This estimation of covariation is consistent with the existing literature. For example, the largest study of concordance in infancy found an intraclass correlation coefficient of .23 (van IJzendoorn et al., 2000). In some respects, the consistency between the estimation and empirical estimation is reassuring. At the same time, several aspects of these findings should not be reassuring.

First, the magnitude of the relations is moderate or even just modest. Parental representations of attachment account for only 25 percent of the variance in infant attachment; approximately 5 percent of the variance in sibling attachment is shared. These estimations can be misleadingly low because of attenuation due to measurement error. For example, if attachment should be conceptualized as a set of continuous variables (Fraley & Spiker, 2003), then simple secure-insecure dichotomizations or the use of discrete categories will underestimate the degree of association with other variables (MacCallum, Zhang, & Preacher, 2002). Yet both the AAI and the

Strange Situation are relatively reliable measures (see Hesse, 1999; Solomon & George, 1999). Accordingly, statistical corrections for attenuation in the relation between parental representations and attachment security would still leave the majority of the variance unaccounted for.

The moderate effect sizes could reflect the fact that attachment security is determined by multiple factors, and consequently a single factor is unlikely to account for much variance (see Ahadi & Diener, 1989). This explanation is appealing, as it seems highly likely that almost all human behavior is multiply determined. Yet factors other than parental sensitivity have not received as much attention as we believe is warranted. Moreover, when other variables are considered, such as parental resources, personality, psychopathology, the marital relationship, social support, or stress (see Belsky, 1999), their influence on infant attachment is commonly explained in terms of the impact on the quality of caregiving, which affects infant security. What is needed is further attention to factors that have their influence other than by affecting parental sensitivity.

The other disturbing aspect of the pattern of findings is that the degree of concordance in sibling attachment can be fully accounted for by parental representations. That is, the estimated covariation ($r = .24$) is what would be expected from a model with just parental representations predicting infant attachment. What might account for this pattern of relations? One possibility is that no other factor contributes to sibling attachment convergence except parental representations. Although possible, it seems unlikely that any single variable would be responsible for determining sibling concordance or any variable reflecting relationship qualities.

Alternatively, another variable may contribute, but its influence is being spuriously attributed to parental representations because that variable covaries with parental representations. Interestingly, a gap in the transmission of attachment patterns from parent to infant has been identified (van IJzendoorn, 1995). That is, some of the effect of a parent's representation on the infant's subsequent attachment can be explained by paths A and B in our model, but approximately 77 percent of the effect remains unexplained. When investigators have tried to account for the transmission gap, they have typically looked for variables other than maternal sensitivity that may mediate the link between parental representations and attachment security. For example, parental mind-mindedness and reflective functioning have been proposed as mediators (Fonagy, Gergely, Jurist, & Target, 2002; Meins, 1999). Although evidence for these mediators exists (Bernier & Dozier, 2003; Slade, Grienenberger, Bernbach, Levy, & Locker, 2005), little consideration has been given to the possibility that it is not a mediator but some covariate of parental representations that is a determinant of infant security and accounts for the seeming transmission gap. The quality of the marital or spousal partnership is one possible covariate. Specifically, the quality of marriage is associated with both representations of attachment and parental caregiving. A harmonious marriage may lead to more secure representations and a more positive child-rearing context for children, providing a sense of safety and security to the infant. Disharmony in the marital relationship could lead to insecurity and poor parenting (see Cox, Paley, & Harter, 2001; Treboux, Crowell, & Waters, 2004). Accordingly, part of the unexplained link between parental representations and attachment security may stem from the fact that both are influenced by the marital relationship.

Finally, it is possible that other variables contribute to concordance in sibling attachment security, but their influence is not apparent because they are offset by another set of variables that lead to discordance in attachment security. Given that siblings share half of their genes, one might expect genetic factors to contribute to concordance in sibling attachment. However, genetic influences appear to play a small role in security of attachment (Bokhorst et al., 2003; van IJzendoorn et al., 2000). Although early reviews and research tended to dismiss the significance of shared environmental influences, more recent work finds evidence of such influences (see Rutter, 2000). As yet, however, the shared environmental factors contributing to concordance in attachment have not been delineated.

Perhaps the more interesting question is what nonshared environmental factors could contribute to differences in attachment security. One possibility is that parents' representations of attachment have different effects on the security of attachment of different siblings. Although relatively stable, a parent's representation could change as a function of having children. Experiences with one's firstborn child could influence one's representation and one's subsequent caregiving behaviors with another child, thus predicting different parenting practices for two siblings raised in the same family. The birth of a sibling may also change the frequency, nature, and context of interactions between parents and existing children, which could have a direct impact on parent-child attachment relationships. In fact, the attachment security of firstborn children is more unstable or tends to decrease after the birth of a sibling (Teti, Sakin, Kucera, Corns, & Eiden, 1996; Touris, Kromelow, & Harding, 1995).

Although it would be important to examine temporal changes in parents' representations of attachment as a function of having children, this is not likely to be the primary explanation of siblings' discordance in attachment. If it were, we would expect concordance to be much greater in twins than siblings because twins would experience the same parental representation as they were born simultaneously. The degree of attachment concordance in monozygotic and dizygotic same-sex twins, however, is not stronger than the concordance rate in same-sex siblings (Bokhorst et al., 1993, $\kappa = .18$; O'Connor & Croft, 2001, $\kappa = .24$; van IJzendoorn et al., 2000, $\kappa = .13$). Similarly, our data did not implicate age spacing as a significant moderator of attachment concordance in adolescent siblings.

Another possibility is that a parent's representations of relationships with his or her own parents interact with the characteristics of the infant to produce unique patterns of attachment across siblings. Investigators have tried to identify child characteristics, such as temperament, that are predictive of attachment security; however, less attention has been paid to the moderating effect of child characteristics on a parent's representations (Belsky, 1997).

Parents' representations of attachment to their own parents may also not be the most proximal mechanism of their caregiving behavior (see Mayseless, 2006). Representations of relationships can be conceptualized in terms of a hierarchical model (Collins & Read, 1990; Furman & Simon, 1999). That is, individuals may have representations of particular relationships, types of relationships (such as romantic relationships), and close relationships in general. Thus, parents may have representations of their relationships with particular children, and these may be stronger predictors of caregiving. In fact, several measures of such representations have been developed and found to be related to AAIs and caregiving behavior (George & Solomon, 1996; Slade, Belsky, Aber, & Phelps, 1999; Zeanah & Benoit, 1995). It seems quite possible that parents have different representations of their relationships with different children and that such representations lead to differential caregiving of their different children and siblings' discordant attachment classifications.

Adolescents' Concordance of Representations

In our study of the concordance of adolescent siblings' attachment representations, we obtained a kappa of .07, whereas in the largest study of infant attachment concordance (van IJzendoorn et al., 2000), the concordance was .23. This difference is not statistically significant, though the chances are slightly greater that it is different than it is not. In effect, we cannot conclude they are the same or different.

In either case, each of the potential explanations for the relatively low level of concordance in infant attachment relationships could contribute to the low concordance observed in adolescent representations. Moreover, several other factors specific to later childhood or adolescence may contribute to the low level of concordance found.

In particular, attachment relationships and representations are hypothesized to be relatively stable, but not completely. In fact, the terminology of "working" and "model" was favored by Bowlby because they suggest processes that are ultimately dynamic and alterable (Bretherton, 1993). Consistent with this idea, security in infant attachment has been predictive of late adolescent representations of attachments to parents in several studies (Hamilton, 2000; Waters, Merrick, Treboux, Crowell, & Albersheim, 2000), but not always (Lewis, Feiring, & Rosenthal, 2000; Weinfield, Sroufe, & Egeland, 2000). Such discontinuity has been linked to negative life events and circumstances, suggesting that there may be lawful discontinuities that lead to changes in attachments and, perhaps, differences in adolescent siblings' attachments (see Chapter Six, this volume).

As children get older, their attachment relationships become increasingly characterized as goal-corrected partnerships (Bowlby, 1969; Waters, Kondo-Ikemura, Posada, & Richters, 1991), and the active role of the child or adolescent increases. Attachment theorists have suggested that the characteristics of the only infant play a small role in infant attachment (Sroufe, 1985; Ward et al., 1988), but the individual characteristics of an adolescent may be more important because of the role he or she plays in determining the relationship with a parent.

Nonshared environmental influences may contribute to discordance in infants' attachment and seem likely to be increasingly important factors as children get older and become adolescents. Consistent with this idea, twins become increasingly less similar as they grow older (McCartney, Harris, & Benieri, 1990). One such nonshared environmental influence that has been thought important is differential parental treatment. The degree of parenting consistency varies considerably as a function of the particular aspect of parenting being examined, but often the consistency is only modest in scope (Furman & Lanthier, 2002) and thus could contribute to differences in siblings' attachment. Much of the literature on parental treatment, however, has focused on objective differences in parenting patterns. One would not expect a sensitive parent to treat children or adolescents of different ages the same; similarly, sometimes practices with a child who is of a particular age would not be as effective or appropriate for another child of that same age (Furman & Lanthier, 2002). The links between differential parenting behaviors and siblings' attachment will require careful consideration of the context of parenting. For example, whether differential treatment is perceived to be fair matters (Kowal, Krull, & Kramer, 2004). Differential parental treatment perceived to be unfair is associated with poorer parent-child relationships, but not differential treatment seen as fair. Moreover, it will be important to provide direct evidence of the role of particular differences in parenting and not simply infer that such differences are important. For example, differences in maternal sensitivity have not been found to be predictive of discordance in attachment security (van IJzendoorn et al., 2000).

Another source of nonshared environmental factors is the interaction between siblings, particularly when one is substantially older than the other. Siblings may also seek to differentiate themselves from each other and counter some of their shared experiences or commonalities in the parenting they have received (Caspi, Herbener, & Ozer, 1992).

Other potential nonshared environmental influences include accidental factors and extrafamilial influences, such as peer and teacher relations (Rowe & Plomin, 1981). To illustrate, one adolescent in our study experienced the loss of a close friend, which significantly affected her expectations of close relationships in general, and hence her classification, but this person's sibling was not directly affected by this loss and was classified differently. To account for cases such as these, we need to develop theoretical models describing the mechanisms by which these extraneous variables have an influence on attachment security, as well as empirical evidence that they are relevant.

It is interesting to note that the degree of concordance in the ratings of loving behavior, especially by mothers, tended to be higher than the concordance in the AAI classifications. Such a finding is particularly striking as both ratings of relationships and the classifications were derived from the AAI. If representations of a relationship were exclusively based on experiences in a relationship as they are believed to be in childhood, we may have expected similar levels of concordance. However, adolescents are able to reflect on their relationship and how it functions (Main et al., 1985). Thus, two adolescent siblings may reflect differently on their experiences with a parent and have different representations of the relationship even if they had similar experiences with a parent. For example, one pair of adolescents in our study shared the experience of a loss but appeared to respond in different ways. The difference in reaction seems to have contributed to their discordance in their representations (one sibling was classified as insecure, the other as secure).

In addition, the process of coalescing representations of particular relationships into an integrated representation of relationships with parents may reduce the degree of concordance. Adolescents' representations of relationships with mothers and fathers are related, but only moderately so (Furman & Simon, 2004). An adolescent may have a secure representation of his or her relationship with one parent and an insecure representation of his or her relationship with the other parent. Moreover, one child may be more influenced by experiences with the mother, whereas the other sibling may be more influenced by experiences with the father. Thus, their generalized representations of their parents may be differentially influenced by the two relationships each has had. Even if each parent behaved consistently toward the two, the siblings' integrated representation of these relationships may not be fully concordant.

In our study of adolescent concordance, we found initial evidence that concordance in attachment appears to be greater when the two siblings both indicated that they were closer to the same parent or equally close to both parents. Future work with a larger sample is necessary to replicate this finding; it would be particularly interesting to compare the concordance in representations of attachment with both parents and concordance in representations of particular parents. If part of the reason for the modest concordance in representations is that siblings incorporate the representations of mothers and fathers differently in their overall representations of relationships with parents, then greater concordance may occur in the specific models of parents. If the modest concordance primarily reflects differences in representations of each parent, then we might expect similar modest levels of concordance in parent-specific representations.

More generally, one of the overarching themes of this volume is the question of the convergence and diversity of adolescents' representations or working models (see Chapter One, this volume). As noted previously, representations of relationships can be conceptualized in terms of a hierarchical model with representations of particular relationships, types of relationships, and close relationships in general (Collins & Read, 1990; Furman & Simon, 1999). As yet, we know relatively little about what contexts elicit which types of representations. Moreover, the relevant representations may also differ as a function of the nature of parental relationships. In a family with no father figure available in adolescents' lives, representations of the relationship with mothers might be particularly salient. In a blended family in which adolescents may be subject to stepparent influences as well as parental influences, the nature of representations may also differ. Further work is needed in understanding differences in representations and what determines the salience of various representations.

Conclusion

In summary, we drew on fundamental principles of attachment to propose a simple model of attachment concordance in adolescent sibling pairs. A review of existing data with children revealed a modest to moderate level of concordance in attachment security; similarly, our own data on adolescents did not find any concordance in representations. These findings are troubling both because they suggest only a moderate or perhaps just modest level of concordance exists, and this concordance can be fully accounted for by parental representations of attachment. We discussed several explanations for this pattern of results and suggested a number of possible paths that could be included in a revised model of adolescent siblings' concordance of attachment. Moreover, we discussed the implications the body of findings has for attachment theory more generally. It is our hope that our examination of the facets and evidence of a simple model of concordance will lead to some new directions for research in this area.

References

Ahadi, S., & Diener, E. (1989). Multiple determinants and effect sizes. *Journal of Personality and Social Psychology, 56,* 398–406.

Ainsworth, M.D.S., Blehar, M., Waters, E., & Wall, S. (1978). *Patterns of attachment: A psychological study of the Strange Situation.* Mahwah, NJ: Erlbaum.

Ammaniti, M., Speranza, A. M., & Candelori, C. (1996). Stability of attachment in children and intergenerational transmission of attachment. *Psichiatria dell'Infancia e dell'Adolescenza, 63,* 313–332.

Belsky, J. (1997). Theory testing, effect-size evaluation, and differential susceptibility to rearing influence: The case of mothering and attachment. *Child Development, 68,* 598–600.

Belsky, J. (1999). Interactional and contextual determinants of attachment security. In J. Cassidy & P. R. Shaver (Eds.), *Handbook of attachment: Theory, research and clinical applications* (pp. 249–264). New York: Guilford Press.

Bernier, A., & Dozier, M. (2003). Bridging the attachment transmission gap: The role of maternal mind-mindedness. *International Journal of Behavioral Development, 27*, 355–365.

Bokhorst, C. L., Bakermans-Kranenburg, M. J., Fearon, R. M., van IJzendoorn, M. H., Fonagy, P., & Schuengel, C. (2003). The importance of shared environment in mother-infant attachment security: A behavioral genetic study. *Child Development, 74*, 1769–1782.

Bowlby, J. (1969). *Attachment and loss: Vol. 1. Attachment.* New York: Basic Books.

Bowlby, J. (1973). *Attachment and loss: Vol. 2. Separation: Anger and Anxiety.* New York: Basic Books.

Bowlby, J. (1980). *Attachment and loss: Vol. 3. Loss: Sadness and depression.* New York: Basic Books.

Bretherton, I. (1985). Attachment theory: Retrospect and prospect. In I. Bretherton & E. Waters (Eds.), Growing points of attachment theory and research. *Monographs of the Society for Research in Child Development, 50* (1–2, Serial No. 209), 3–35.

Bretherton, I. (1993). From dialogue to internal working models: The co-construction of self in relationships. In C. A. Nelson (Ed.), *Minnesota Symposia in Child Psychology: Vol. 26. Memory and affect in development* (pp. 237–263). Mahwah, NJ: Erlbaum.

Caspi, A., Herbener, E. S., & Ozer, D. J. (1992). Shared experiences and the similarity of personalities: A longitudinal study of married couples. *Journal of Personality and Social Psychology, 62*, 281–291.

Collins, N. L., & Read, S. J. (1990). Adult attachment, working models, and relationship quality in dating couples. *Journal of Personality and Social Psychology, 58*, 644–663.

Cox, M. J., Paley, B., & Harter, K. (2001). Interparental conflict and parent-child relationships. In J. Grych & F. Fincham (Eds.), *Child development and interparental conflict* (pp 249–272). Cambridge: Cambridge University Press.

Crowell, J. A., Treboux, D., & Waters, E. (2002). Stability of attachment representations: The transition to marriage. *Developmental Psychology, 38*, 467–479.

De Wolff, M., & van IJzendoorn, M. H. (1997). Sensitivity and attachment: A meta-analysis on parental antecedents of infant attachment. *Child Development, 68*, 571–591.

Fonagy, P., Gergely, G., Jurist, E. L., & Target, M. (2002). *Affect regulation, mentalization, and the development of the self.* New York: Other Press.

Fraley, R. C., & Spieker, S. J. (2003). Are infant attachment patterns continuously or categorically distributed? A taxometric analysis of strange situation behavior. *Developmental Psychology, 39*, 387–404.

Furman, W., & Lanthier, R. (2002). Parenting siblings. In M. Bornstein (Ed.), *Handbook of parenting: Vol. 1. Children and parenting* (2nd ed., pp. 165–188). Mahwah, NJ: Erlbaum.

Furman, W., & Simon, V. A. (1999). Cognitive representations of adolescent romantic relationships. In W. Furman, B. B. Brown, & C. Feiring (Eds.), *The development of romantic relationships in adolescence* (pp. 75–98). Cambridge: Cambridge University Press.

Furman, W., & Simon, V. A. (2004). Concordance in attachment states of mind and styles with respect to fathers and mothers. *Developmental Psychology, 40*, 1239–1247.

Furman, W., & Wehner, E. A. (1994). Romantic views: Toward a theory of adolescent romantic relationships. In R. Montmayer, G. R. Adams, & G. P. Gullota (Eds.), *Advances in adolescent development: Vol. 6. Personal relationships during adolescence* (pp. 168–175). Thousand Oaks, CA: Sage.

George, C., Kaplan, N., & Main, M. (1985). *Adult Attachment Interview.* Unpublished manuscript, University of California, Berkeley, CA.

George, C., & Solomon, J. (1996). Representational models of relationships: Links between caregiving and attachment. *Infant Mental Health Journal, 17*, 198–216.

Hamilton, C. E. (2000). Continuity and discontinuity of attachment from infancy through adolescence. *Child Development, 71*, 690–694.

Hazan, C., & Zeifman, D. (1994). Sex and the psychological tether. In K. Bartholomew & D. Perlman (Eds.), *Advances in personal relationships: Vol. 5. Attachment processes in adulthood* (pp. 151–178). London: Jessica Kingsley.

Hesse, E. (1999). The Adult Attachment Interview: Historical and current perspectives. In J. Cassidy & P. R. Shaver (Eds.), *Handbook of attachment theory and research* (pp. 395–433). New York: Guilford Press.

Kowal, A. K., Krull, J. L., & Kramer, L. (2004). How the differential treatment of siblings is linked with parent-child relationship quality. *Journal of Family Psychology, 18,* 658–665.

Lewis, M., Feiring, C. & Rosenthal, S. (2000). Attachment over time. *Child Development, 7,* 707–720.

Loehlin, J. (2004). *Latent variable models: An introduction to factor, path, and structural equation models* (4th ed.). Mahwah, NJ: Erlbaum.

MacCallum, R. C., Zhang, S., & Preacher, K. J. (2002). On the practice of dichotomization of quantitative variables. *Psychological Methods, 7,* 19–40.

Main, M. (1999). Epilogue: Attachment theory: Eighteen points with suggestions for future studies. In J. Cassidy & P. R. Shaver (Eds.), *Handbook of attachment: Theory, research and clinical applications* (pp. 845–888). New York: Guilford Press.

Main, M., & Goldwyn, R. (1984). *Adult attachment scoring and classification systems.* Unpublished manuscript, University of California at Berkeley.

Main, M., Kaplan, N., & Cassidy, J. (1985). Security in infancy, childhood, and adulthood: A move to the level of representation. In I. Bretherton & E. Waters (Eds.), Growing points of attachment theory and research. *Monographs of the Society for Research in Child Development, 50* (1–2, Serial No. 209), 66–106.

Mayseless, O. (Ed.). (2006). *Studying parenting representations as a window to parents' internal working model of caregiving.* Cambridge: Cambridge University Press.

McCartney, K., Harris, M. J., & Benieri, F. (1990). Growing up and growing apart: A developmental meta-analysis of twin studies. *Psychological Bulletin, 107,* 226–237.

Meins, E. (1999). Sensitivity, security, and internal working models: Bridging the transmission gap. *Attachment and Human Development, 1,* 325–342.

O'Connor, T. G., & Croft, C. M. (2001). A twin study of attachment in preschool children. *Child Development, 72,* 1501–1511.

Rowe, D. C., & Plomin, R. (1981). The importance of nonshared (E1) environmental influences in behavioral development. *Developmental Psychology, 17,* 517–531.

Rutter, M. (2000). Psychosocial influences: Critiques, findings, and research needs. *Development and Psychopathology, 12,* 375–405.

Slade, A., Belsky, J., Aber, J. L., & Phelps, J. L. (1999). Mothers' representations of their relationships with their toddlers: Links to adult attachment and observed mothering. *Developmental Psychology, 35,* 611–619.

Slade, A., Grienenberger, J., Bernbach, E., Levy, D., & Locker, A. (2005). Maternal reflective functioning, attachment, and the transmission gap: A preliminary study. *Attachment and Human Development, 7,* 283–298.

Solomon, J., & George, C. (1999). The measurement of attachment security in infancy and childhood. In J. Cassidy & P. R. Shaver (Eds.), *Handbook of attachment theory and research* (pp. 287–318). New York: Guilford Press.

Sroufe, L. A. (1985). Attachment classification from the perspective of infant-caregiver relationships and infant temperament. *Child Development, 56,* 1–14.

Teti, D. M., Sakin, J., Kucera, E., Corns, K. M., & Eiden, R. D. (1996). And baby makes four: Predictors of attachment security among preschool-aged firstborns during the transition to siblinghood. *Child Development, 67,* 579–596.

Touris, M., Kromelow, S., & Harding, C. (1995). Mother-firstborn attachment and the birth of a sibling. *American Journal of Orthopsychiatry, 65,* 293–297.

Treboux, D., Crowell, J. A., & Waters, E. (2004). When "new" meets "old": Configurations of adult attachment representations and their implications for marital functioning. *Developmental Psychology, 40,* 295–314.

Van IJzendoorn, M. (1995). Adult attachment representations, parental responsiveness, and infant attachment on the predictive validity of the Adult Attachment Interview. *Psychological Bulletin, 117,* 387–403.

Van IJzendoorn, M., Moran, G., Belsky, J., Pederson, D., Bakermans-Kranenburg, M. J., & Kneppers, K. (2000). The similarity of siblings' attachments to their mother. *Child Development, 71*, 1086–1098.

Ward, M., Vaughn, B. E., & Robb, M. D. (1988). Social-emotional adaptation and infant-mother attachment in siblings: Role of the mother in cross-sibling consistency. *Child Development, 59*, 643–651.

Waters, E., Kondo-Ikemura, K., Posada, G., & Richters, J. E. (1991). Learning to love: Mechanisms and milestones. In M. R. Gunnar & L. A. Sroufe (Eds.), *Self processes and development* (pp. 217–255). Mahwah, NJ: Erlbaum.

Waters, E., Merrick, C., Treboux, D., Crowell, J., & Albersheim, L. (2000). Attachment security in infancy and early adulthood: A twenty-year longitudinal study. *Child Development, 71*, 684–689.

Weinfield, N. S., Sroufe, A. L., & Egeland, B. (2000). Attachment from infancy to early adulthood in a high-risk sample: Continuity, discontinuity, and their correlates. *Child Development, 71*, 695–702.

Zeanah, C. H., & Benoit, D. (1995). Clinical applications of a parent perception interview in infant mental health. *Child and Adolescent Psychiatric Clinics of North America, 4*, 539–554.

LISA KIANG is assistant professor of psychology at Wake Forest University, Winston-Salem, North Carolina.

WYNDOL FURMAN is a John Evans Professor at the University of Denver.

6

Longitudinal research in a risk sample reaffirms the importance of the construct of adolescent attachment and provides important clues to sources of variation during development.

Adolescent Attachment Representations and Development in a Risk Sample

Jill Carlivati, W. Andrew Collins

There is ample evidence that close relationships are the sine qua non of social life from birth to old age (Reis, Collins, & Berscheid, 2000). In developmental perspective, attachment is the theoretical construct that most clearly embodies an understanding that early relationships exert influence on later ones. Although developmentalists have benefited from the solid theoretical and empirical base on caregiver-infant relationships, increasingly there is a need to examine the key indicators of the attachment construct in the context of adolescent development (Allen & Land, 1999; Main, Kaplan, & Cassidy, 1985).

The focus of this chapter is continuity and change in attachment representations in a sample at risk because of early poverty. Our particular emphasis is adolescence and reasons that adolescence may be a period of attachment security change in the at-risk population. We begin with an overview of key issues in adolescent attachment, reflecting conclusions drawn from the relatively small literature. With this background, we examine attachment stability and change in a risk sample of individuals followed from birth to age twenty-eight, the at-risk sample of the Minnesota Longitudinal Study of Risk and Adaptation, proposing explanations for the observed patterns of relationship behaviors with varied partners from infancy to adulthood. In the final section, we outline some features of a

NEW DIRECTIONS FOR CHILD AND ADOLESCENT DEVELOPMENT, no. 117, Fall 2007 © Wiley Periodicals, Inc.
Published online in Wiley InterScience (www.interscience.wiley.com) • DOI: 10.1002/cd.196

framework for future research on attachment in the heterogeneous adolescent population.

Attachment from Infancy to Adolescence

Attachment in infant-caregiver relationships refers to a relatively unique or distinct interpersonal connection that supports the regulation of emotions and feelings of safety from threatening conditions. These internal emotional experiences are manifested in the organization of the infant's behavior to maintain proximity with the caregiver, especially in novel or threatening circumstances. Infants may feel secure with multiple partners, though these relationships may vary in the degree to which the infant feels secure in them (Cassidy, 1999; Weinfield, Sroufe, Egeland, & Carlson, 1999).

Maintaining interdependence in adolescence and early adulthood occasions multiple opportunities for reassuring connections with others. Adolescents' perceptions of parents as primary sources of support generally decline, whereas perceived support from peers increases, such that peers are seen as providing roughly the same (Helsen, Vollebergh, & Meeus, 2000; Scholte, van Lieshout, & van Aken, 2001) or greater (Furman & Buhrmester, 1992) support as parents. This is especially evident with friends and romantic interests, the individuals with whom adolescents are most likely to spend time (proximity seeking) and with whom they most want to be when feeling vulnerable (safe haven function) (Ainsworth, 1989; Cassidy, 2001; Waters & Cummings, 2000). During adolescence, attachment is transformed from caregiving of one partner by the other to that of mutual caregiving between the two partners (Allen & Land, 1999; Cassidy, 2001; Waters & Cummings, 2000).

Findings provide compelling evidence that secure adolescent attachment representations are associated with positive social experiences and relationships and optimal development of social skills in both early adolescence (Allen, Marsh, McFarland, McElhaney, Land, Jodl, et al., 2002) and later adolescence (Kobak & Sceery, 1988). Such data imply normative stability in relationships mediated by representations. In current parent-child relationships, adolescents with secure representations displayed intellectual and emotional autonomy in interactions with mothers, when the mothers were sensitive and supportive to adolescents' assertions of autonomy (Allen et al., 2003). Such adolescents also manifested concurrent competence with peers; secure representations were related directly to peer popularity and self-esteem and inversely to depression and delinquency (Allen, Moore, Kuperminc, & Bell, 1998). Prediction from representations was even stronger for positive qualities of friendships than for general peer competence (Zimmermann, 2004). Individuals with secure representations were less anxious and less hostile, dismissing participants were more hostile, and preoccupied participants were more anxious and distressed. Moreover, attachment representation security has been linked to greater consonance between facial emotion expression and self-rating of emotions during cooperative problem-solving interactions with friends (Zimmermann, Maier, Winter, & Grossmann, 2001). Adolescents with insecure representations also were more likely to behave disruptively when faced with confusion, helplessness, disappointment, and resignation. This pattern parallels emotion-regulation differences between insecure and secure participants generally (Zimmermann et al., 2001).

Continuity and Change. Several researchers have documented remarkable correspondence between Adult Attachment Interview (AAI) classifications (George, Kaplan, & Main, 1985) and an individual's actual manifestations of security in relationships with caregivers in infancy (Waters, Weinfield, & Hamilton, 2000) and also representations of romantic relationships, as assessed by the Current Relationships Interview (CRI; Crowell & Owens, 1996). Although continuity within the adolescent period has rarely been studied, Allen, McElhaney, Kuperminc, and Jodl (2004) reported substantial two-year stability from middle to late adolescence, and a meta-analysis by van IJzendoorn and Bakermans-Kranenburg (1996) showed a statistically similar distribution of attachment classifications for adolescent as opposed to adult samples.

Change is both plausible and evident, as well. Ammaniti, van IJzendoorn, Speranza, and Tambelli (2000) found that while rank-ordering of individuals by security (using a dimension of security to insecurity) is similar over development, with the most secure individuals remaining more secure relative to peers over time, more frequent and intense rejection, derogation, and lack of recall are reported in early adolescence relative to late adolescence. Dismissing representations were especially likely during this early period. In higher-risk samples, similar increases in rejection, derogation, and lack of recall may result in larger numbers of adolescents, with scores on the border between security and insecurity. These adolescents may be especially likely to make the transition to dismissing representations, thus affecting the attachment distribution (Weinfield, Sroufe, & Egeland, 2000). Moreover, the possibility of greater insight and ability to rationalize and integrate experiences may make change to security possible during adolescence. Allen et al. (2004) found such increases in security during adolescence in a low-risk subsample of adolescents.

Accounting for Discontinuity. Attempts to account for changes in attachment security have largely emphasized normative changes of the period. Cognitive abilities are key to comprehending the internalization of experience into representation (Carlson, Sroufe, & Egeland, 2004). Attachment security is realized in the context of the adolescent's abilities to understand and compare abstract relationship concepts (Allen & Land, 1999; Bretherton, 1985; Main et al., 1985; Thompson, 2000; Waters & Cummings, 2000; Waters, Kondo-Ikemura, Posada, & Richters, 1991). Thus, differences in representation at adolescence could be accounted for in part by cognitive changes of adolescence (see Chapter Three, this volume, for additional thoughts on the attachment-information processing link). As cognitive abilities increase, the individual begins to develop the capacity to assess others' intentions and motives, and his or her coping skills increase (Bretherton, 1985). Cognitive advances should enhance the ability of adolescents to process information about relationships and better understand their experiences (Bretherton & Munholland, 1999; Furman & Simon, 1999). In fact, Main et al. (1985) have argued that this level of cognitive sophistication may be necessary for representational change. Normative revision of attachment-related information should correspond to greater access to thoughts, feelings, memories, and aspects of the self, which could enhance the effectiveness of interventions and clinical applications of attachment (Scott Brown & Wright, 2003).

Despite the promise of cognitive explanations, the influence and application of new cognitive abilities may not produce effective analysis and revision of all representations. For example, Furman and Simon (1999) argue that perspective taking in romantic relationships should lag behind that in parent-child relationships. Self-consciousness in an unfamiliar relationship domain, as well as the infatuation component of romantic relationships, is hypothesized to delay progress in revising these representations as cognitive changes occur (Furman & Simon, 1999).

Changing relationships with parents may provide a more satisfactory explanation for changes in adolescent attachment representations. One source of change is the normative press for greater autonomy during adolescence. Although parents serve as safe havens throughout the period (Allen & Land, 1999; Collins, 1995, 1997; Hunter & Youniss, 1982), strained communication, physical inaccessibility, and inhibited responsiveness may become more prevalent as families attempt to balance the complementary dimensions of autonomy and relatedness (Allen & Hauser, 1996; Kobak, 1999). Establishing autonomy should be easier for adolescents with secure models, as through the process there is confidence in the parent-child relationship; with insecure adolescents, autonomy establishment is threatening to the dyad, making the process more strained (Allen & Land, 1999). Changes to security corresponding to increased autonomy may reflect more thorough analyses of attachment relationships and figures as adolescents experience more distance from their parents. It should be noted, however, that the powerful push for autonomy may make it difficult to detect security during adolescence (Allen & Land, 1999).

Another parent-child relationship change is that in the child's view of the parents during adolescence. Adolescents may either idealize or devalue their parents in attempts to distance themselves as they strive for autonomy, reflected in increased numbers of dismissing attachment representations (Ammaniti et al., 2000). The short lag between childhood and early adolescence allows little time for consolidating this new perspective on parents, and this foreshortened process may account for fewer secure representations in adolescence than in earlier and later periods (see Sampson, 2004, for findings in an at-risk sample). An important caveat comes from Allen et al.'s finding (2004) that adolescent deidealization did not predict change in security during adolescence, raising the possibility that security may affect deidealization rather than the reverse direction of effect.

Clearly, however, childhood dependency on a parent and ongoing physical proximity may interfere with exploration of the attachment relationship during adolescence. Fully and rationally acknowledging the faults of a relationship when living with parents is likely to be difficult. Parent-child conflict patterns over adolescence may also account for security change. A meta-analysis reveals that rates of conflict decrease while the affect in conflicts increases during adolescence (Laursen, Coy, & Collins, 1998). Hence, the conflict may stimulate change in attachment representations because more intense yet less frequent interactions during adolescence possibly lead to greater questioning of one's relationship.

Denying current negative effects of the relationship should interfere with the ability to gain autonomy in representation (Waters, Hamilton, & Weinfield, 2000). Individuals with dismissing representations in adolescence or early adulthood may be able to make the transition to or "reclaim their security" if eventual development and distance from parents allow them to explore their experiences and gain coherence (Weinfield et al., 2000, p. 703). In addition, Treboux, Crowell, and Waters (2004) question whether the developmental tasks of late adolescence, such as leaving home, could temporarily change representations, raising the possibility that idealization may occur during such transitions for individuals otherwise unlikely to idealize. Thus far, however, findings from research on the impact of leaving home, though informative about moderating factors, have left open the significance of coresidence for representations of security (Mayseless, 2004; Scharf, Mayseless, & Kivenson-Baron, 2004; Scharf & Mayseless, 2005).

Research on change in attachment during adolescence is still in its infancy, although findings are accumulating on continuity in attachment and correlates of various representations. The challenge of understanding how multiple relationship representations form, their relations to one another, and the impact on development is a key challenge for future research.

The Minnesota Longitudinal Study of Risk and Adaptation. Many of the preceding generalizations about adolescent attachment are based on samples of relatively well-functioning middle-class adolescents. Little is known about whether, how, and with what significance attachment representations might differ across subsamples that vary in social class, ethnicity, culture, and other groups. The remaining sections of the chapter examine the potential significance of attachment in a sample in which socioemotional functioning is less consistently high. Data from such a sample may further illuminate the significant conditions and processes in attachment during adolescence.

The Minnesota Longitudinal Study of Risk and Adaptation is a study designed for identifying and examining developmental influences and processes (Sroufe, Egeland, Carlson, & Collins, 2005a). The study began in 1976 as a prospective study of high-risk children and their families. Today it has become a multifaceted investigation with a persistent dual focus: an emphasis on normative development and the quality of environmental supports necessary for optimal adaptation.

The sample initially had 267 mothers who were at risk for poor-quality caregiving because of poverty and associated risk factors. Currently 180 of their children, born in 1976 and 1977, still participate in data collection. Of the current participants, 69 percent are Caucasian, 11 percent are African American, 4 percent are Native American, and 16 percent are mixed race. The risk status of the sample has been confirmed in a variety of ways. At age nineteen, 23 percent of the sample had dropped out of school, 11 percent had been incarcerated, and 32 percent had reported problems with drugs and alcohol (for example, arrests for drunk driving). Thirty-six percent received a diagnosis of a current DSM-III-R disorder (61 percent lifetime prevalence) based on the K-SADS interview at age seventeen and a half. From ages eighteen to twenty-three, 208 official offenses were committed by sixty-six adults. At age twenty-six, 61 percent had been unemployed at some point in the three previous years, and 21 percent had engaged in criminal activity between the ages of twenty-four and twenty-six years. By contrast, some participants were doing well: 16 percent of the participants had earned a four-year college degree or better, and 16 percent had earned a two-year college, technical, or business school degree. At the twenty-six-year assessment, 76 percent of the sample was working, and 71 percent had held a full-time job at some point in the previous three years. By 2005, the participants manifested a spectrum of individual differences in normative development, from the most competent and resilient individuals to those who show the most adaptational failure (Sroufe et al., 2005a).

Several features of the research are distinctive. First, the investigators assessed the participants frequently and extensively; subsamples were studied in preschool, middle childhood, adolescence, and early adulthood. Second, in each developmental period, information was gathered on the child and on parental characteristics and caregiving skills, child behaviors, interactions with others, and environmental circumstances. Third, assessments have included multiple independent measures. Finally, the research has emphasized developmentally keyed focal constructs or patterns of adaptation with respect to the salient issues of a given developmental period (Sroufe et al., 2005a).

The focus on developmentally keyed focal constructs reflects the premise that relationships are salient developmental adaptations in each life period (Sroufe, Carlson, & Shulman, 1993). To bring close relationships into this picture, the study included measures of competence in peer relationships in childhood and adolescence, close friendships in adolescence, and romantic relationships in middle and late adolescence and early adulthood.

Ratings of adolescent friendships and romantic relationships came from extensive interviews when participants were ages sixteen, nineteen, and twenty-three. Relationships receiving the highest ratings were characterized by mutual caring, trust, support, and emotional closeness. For those in dating relationships of two months or more (at ages sixteen and nineteen) and four months or more (at age twenty-three), interview responses about romantic relationships were collected. At ages twenty to twenty-one, participants who had been in a self-defined romantic relationship for four months or longer came to the laboratory with their partners for interviewing and observation. Coders achieved a reliability of $r_i = .95$ (intraclass correlation) on ratings of overall relationship quality.

These longitudinal data place adolescent functioning in the context of attachment in early life, late adolescence, and adulthood. Thus far, they have yielded important information about adolescent attachment and its developmental significance. Among the key findings are those related to issues of continuity and change, the value of multiple assessments of attachment, the significance of representation in developmental processes, and the impact of life stress and maltreatment.

Recognizing the Vagaries of Continuity. Studying continuity in a risk sample points to important exceptions in the usual finding of continuity from childhood to adolescence. For example, Weinfield et al. (2000) studied fifty-seven nineteen year olds from the Minnesota sample. The group was chosen because of stable attachment classifications in the Strange Situation from twelve months to eighteen months. Comparing participants' Adult Attachment Interview (AAI) classifications with Strange Situation classifications, these investigators found a continuity rate of 38.6 percent. This rate did not reach statistical significance. Sampson (2004; Sampson & Carlson, 2005) subsequently conducted simple comparisons between infant attachment classifications and AAI scores at age twenty-six. The rate of continuity between these two ages was 37 percent, a figure almost identical to the continuity rate between infancy and age nineteen.

These continuity rates contrast with continuity in studies of relatively well-functioning middle-class, low-risk samples. Waters, Merrick, Treboux, Crowell, and Albersheim (2000), for example, reported 64 percent correspondence across twenty years. The concordance was even higher (72 percent) when only the secure-insecure distinction was used. In accounting for the differences between the two samples, Weinfield et al. (2000) and Weinfield, Whaley, and Egeland (2004) documented that poverty and disruptive life events often undermine continuity in a risk sample. In a related finding, Allen et al. (2004) reported substantial continuity overall, but declines in attachment security for adolescents with enmeshed, overpersonalized behavior with mothers, depressive symptoms, and poverty status. These exceptions are consistent with the hypothesis that current functioning reflects a combination of relationship history and current experiences (Carlson et al., 2004; Sroufe et al., 2005a; for a critical view of these findings, see Lewis, Feiring, & Rosenthal, 2000).

Despite the vagaries of continuity in representations in the risk sample, key provisions of classical attachment views were confirmed in these studies. For example, certain classifications showed concordance across time that would be expected from conceptualizations of attachment categories. Weinfield et al. (2004) and Sampson and Carlson (2005) found that infants whose relationship with caregivers had been classified as disorganized in the Strange Situation were consistently rated as insecure (either unresolved or dismissing) on the AAI in early adulthood. In a later section, we consider evidence for continuities involving assessments of attachment-related constructs other than the AAI.

Incorporating Multiple Assessments of Attachment. The Minnesota Longitudinal Study includes multiple assessments of states of mind related to attachment in adolescence and early adulthood. Besides the AAI, at ages twenty to twenty-two and twenty-six to twenty-seven, participants completed the Current Relationship Interview (CRI; Crowell & Owens, 1996) and self-report inventory measures of adult attachment style. These measures reflect differing approaches to assessment and focus on differing attachment models. In contrast to the AAI focus on states of mind regarding early caregiving experiences, the CRI pertains to state of mind regarding the current relationship with a romantic partner. Measures of adult attachment style—in this case, the Relationship Scales Questionnaire (Griffin & Bartholomew, 1994), which included the Adult Attachment Scale (Collins & Read, 1990)—referred to current relationships, though with a generalized other rather than a specific partner.

To address the question of whether reliance on only the Strange Situation and the AAI might somehow have underestimated the extent of continuity in attachment in earlier analyses, researchers tested for continuity between infancy and these adult measures. Sampson (2003) reported statistically nonsignificant correspondence between infant attachment (Strange Situations at twelve and eighteen months) and the AAI in adulthood. Roisman, Collins, Sroufe, and Egeland (2005) documented interrelations that were more nuanced than the expected one-to-one correspondence across time. Individuals who had been classified as secure in the Strange Situation were more likely than those classified as insecure to produce coherent discourse about their current romantic relationship at ages twenty to twenty-two. That the observed behaviors of the early-secure individuals with their partners were also rated as higher in quality provides convergent validity for the representations of these relationships. In addition, in analyses of hierarchical linear models, Strange Situation classifications predicted CRI classifications over and above observed current relationship quality. In short, findings from the Minnesota Longitudinal Study raise the possibility that representations of current salient relationships, rather than memories of earlier relationships, may be particularly meaningful sequelae of attachment in earlier periods.

Examining Representation and Process. The prototype hypothesis is that representations of relationships are abstracted from dyadic experience and guide both expectations about and observable behavior within future intimate relationships (Collins & Sroufe, 1999; Sroufe & Fleeson, 1986). Analyses of Minnesota Longitudinal Study data have shown that rather than direct transmission from early to late relationships, representations and behavior alike are best predicted by the entire history of experience plus current circumstances (Sroufe et al., 2005a; Sroufe, Egeland, Carlson, & Collins, 2005b). Findings from the study have confirmed that representation carries forward prior experience, framing subsequent encounters with the environment, and in turn being reshaped by these subsequent experiences.

One recent demonstration specifically supported the validity of a dynamic, interactive model to account for these findings. Carlson et al. (2004) examined interrelations among representations of salient relationships from early childhood, middle childhood, and adolescence and assessed representations using age-appropriate and validated assessments. Across childhood and adolescence, current experience predicted subsequent relationship representation, holding prior representation constant; reciprocally, current representation predicted subsequent behavior, holding current behavior constant. This is perhaps the most compelling demonstration to date that representations partly mediate the link between prior experience and later adjustment. Whether the outcome is peer group success in middle childhood and adolescence, romantic relationship quality in early adulthood, or some other specific form of competence, predictions based on cumulative measures of experience and representations strongly predict both continuity and change, whereas predictions from a single indicator, though often significant, consistently emerge as comparatively weaker (Carlson, Jacobvitz, & Sroufe, 1995; Sroufe et al., 2005a; Yates, Egeland, & Sroufe, 2003). An important caveat is Carlson et al.'s finding (2004) of moderate early childhood to midadolescent continuity in relationship representation, but low-middle to late-adolescent continuity. There are several possible reasons for lower continuity in middle to late adolescence. Perhaps any stability found at the group level of analysis masks individual changes in security, similar to the apparent masking observed by Allen et al. (2004). Furthermore, the cognitive and parent-child relationship changes occurring during adolescence outlined above may account for Carlson et al.'s finding (2004). Similarly, uncertainty regarding the transition to adulthood and significant choices regarding adult roles may temporarily strain feelings of security (Arnett, 2000).

Other analyses from the Minnesota Longitudinal Study have revealed that processes by which representation contributes to adaptation at and after adolescence may be more complex than previously recognized. For example, in Roisman et al.'s study (2005) linking infant attachment in the Strange Situation to representations of current romantic relationships using the CRI, the association between infant and romantic security was partly mediated by participants' self-reports about their romantic experiences. Individuals who reported feeling closer to their partners, experiencing positive emotion in interactions, and feeling satisfied with the relationship were more likely to reflect concordance between early relationship security and representations of current romantic partnerships. Thus, the Minnesota data raise the possibility that early experiences may shape later representations by influencing individuals' expectations for and perceptions of love relationships.

The Special Significance of Maltreatment and Life Stress. It is generally expected that early attachment classification would remain stable for most individuals if they experienced stable environments, including relationship qualities, over time (Van IJzendoorn & Bakermans-Kranenburg, 1996). Negative life events may exert their influence through stress on caregiver availability and responsiveness or expectations of these factors, although effects may also be indirect, affecting other family members and stressing the family system as a whole (Waters et al., 2000). Kobak (1999) suggests that stressors such as divorce will impact security when perceived as threats to attachment figure availability. However, Weinfield et al. (2000) found that maternal stress did not account for changes in attachment security in their at-risk sample, suggesting that parental stress explanations may not adequately account for change in adolescents at risk.

Still, stress in the adolescent's life may have strong effects on attachment representation when confounded with the normative stress expected during adolescence. Van IJzendoorn and Bakermans-Kranenburg (1996) in a meta-analysis found higher percentages of dismissing and unresolved AAI classifications for adults from low-socioeconomic (SES) samples, perhaps a reflection of a stressful life turning attention away from attachment concerns. Similar abundance of dismissing participants in low-SES adolescent samples may be hypothesized, especially in the light of additional adolescence-specific stressors.

In the Minnesota Longitudinal Study, individuals whose attachment classifications changed from secure in infancy to insecure at age nineteen were more likely than nonchangers to have been maltreated in childhood, as well as to have experienced maternal depression and conflictual family functioning in early adolescence (Weinfield et al., 2000). In the follow-up with AAI scores at age twenty-six, child maltreatment in early adolescence was correlated with attachment change from infancy to early adulthood (Sampson, 2004). In short, attachment representations can be altered by difficult and chaotic life experiences.

Less acute sources of stress also may contribute to discontinuity in attachment. Such stressors would be expected in the poverty risk sample in the Minnesota Longitudinal Study. Poverty entails diverse stressors, many of which could have been inimical to early security; furthermore, additional stressors would have been likely for many of the participants, in and beyond childhood. Allen et al. (2004) found substantial attachment continuity in a moderately at-risk sample of adolescents; however, when the sample was divided into high- and low-risk groups based on parent-child interaction quality, adolescents' depressive symptoms, and poverty status, those in the high-risk group decreased in security across adolescence, while the low-risk group increased. Stress had overwhelmed the attachment system. The convergence of life stress and normative stressors of the adolescent period may contribute to such disorienting effects. In the Minnesota sample, the most common change pattern was secure-to-dismissing, perhaps reflecting the attenuation of attachment to caregiver hypothesized by other researchers (see Chapters One and Four, this volume, for explanation of the diversification and expansion of attachment figures beyond the caregiver during adolescence).

In a similar vein, Hamilton (2000) showed that divorce occurring during early childhood and with higher levels of parental conflict was associated with secure-to-insecure changes; continuously secure participants who experienced a parental divorce tended to have experienced a less acrimonious parental divorce than those who changed. Lewis et al. (2000), however, found divorce to relate to adolescent attachment representation but not infant attachment security, with no effect of the age of the child at time of parental divorce.

Not all research findings support the role of stressful life events in representational change. Hamilton (2000) found no differences in attachment representation security, negative life events, or infancy-to-adolescent continuity for participants in conventional two-parent homes versus other, presumably more stressful, family structures. Although negative life events were related modestly to discontinuity in attachment representation, these events were more highly associated with early infant insecurity (Hamilton, 2000). Hamilton's results speak to the need to take a full life span developmental approach to adolescent attachment changes rather than investigating adolescence in isolation.

Toward a Framework for Further Research on Attachment in Diverse Adolescents

The Minnesota Longitudinal Study findings and results from the small number of other studies of attachment in risk samples (Allen et al., 2004) underscore contextual and interpersonal conditions that can affect the search for continuity of attachment representations over time. These conditions were not readily apparent in either the germinal formulations of attachment or results from more homogeneous and well-functioning samples. Multiple influences and processes undoubtedly contribute to anomalies in attachment representation or population distributions of attachment classifications during adolescence. Thus, a lengthy agenda looms for future research on continuity in adolescent attachment. Of particular importance are studies designed to account for individual trajectories of change and to avoid masking meaningful group differences when collapsing across age and risk groups.

One point for future clarification in analyses of continuity is the degree to which attachment in infancy and early childhood can be considered prototypical of adolescent relationships. If the interrelation among attachment assessments is expected to be high, then Strange Situation behavior or AAI representations would represent a generalized model of close relationships, relating to a broader range of relationship indicators. At a minimum, research should address relations among attachment models, multifaceted assessments of romantic relationships, friendship, and social support. Carlivati's initial work (2006) on the Minnesota sample implies that AAI representations may not account for romantic relationship behavioral organization. By contrast, the CRI's focus on current romantic partners did predict more strongly than the AAI to observed and reported romantic relationship qualities. Correlates of the CRI are likely to be relatively distinctive from those of the AAI during adolescence. Other work suggests a weak, nonsignificant correspondence between these CRI assessments of security and the AAI-assessed security (Roisman, Madsen, Hennighausen, Sroufe, & Collins, 2001; Roisman et al., 2005). In their comparatively low-risk sample, Owens et al. (1995) also found only modest overlap between AAI and CRI security.

Clarification is needed regarding the relation between the AAI and CRI models, a point also argued by Allen and Manning (Chapter Two, this volume). Theoretically, during late adolescence and early adulthood, representations assessed revealed in both the AAI and CRI may predict observed romantic relationship behavior organization. Based on previous findings, however, a reasonable hypothesis is that the AAI will be relatively more effective than the CRI in predicting friendship and social support ratings, and the CRI will be more effective than the AAI in predicting romantic relationship ratings, during late adolescence and early adulthood (Carlivati, 2006). Perfect correspondence between the AAI and the CRI is not plausible because romantic relationships are distinctive from early parent-child relationships with respect to mutuality in secure base behaviors, including caregiving and care seeking (Bretherton, 1985; Crowell, Fraley, & Shaver, 1999). Whereas high reciprocity of these behaviors may be highly significant in voluntary dyads, such as close friendships and romantic relationships, some forms of mutuality in involuntary relationships, such as caregiving by a child and care seeking by a parent, have potentially negative implications.

Future research involving multiple adolescent representations first requires specifying conceptually expected connections between differing representations, followed by careful examination of the networks of relationships in which an adolescent may experience attachments. Among the questions of interest are whether a hierarchy of representations exists and, if not, whether a horizontal model of attachments is more appropriate. For example, while theoretical perspectives on the relations among numerous attachment representations are emerging (see Chapters One, Two, and Four, this volume), little empirical basis exists for clarifying whether and when a peer representation will attain primacy in the attachment hierarchy or whether a hierarchy is the best way to characterize attachment relationships in adolescence (for initial work in this area, see Carlivati, 2006). In adolescence more than at earlier ages, understanding attachment necessitates understanding the larger context of social development in which relationship presentations are formed and in which they attain significance and continuity across time.

References

Ainsworth, M. S. (1989). Attachments beyond infancy. *American Psychologist, 44*(4), 709–716.

Allen, J. P., & Hauser, S. T. (1996). Autonomy and relatedness in adolescent-family interactions as predictors of young adults' states of mind regarding attachment. *Development and Psychopathology, 8*(4), 793–809.

Allen, J. P., & Land, D. J. (1999). Attachment in adolescence. In J. Cassidy & P. R. Shaver (Eds.), *Handbook of attachment* (pp. 319–335). New York: Guilford Press.

Allen, J. P., Marsh, P., McFarland, C., McElhaney, K. B., Land, D. J., Jodl, K. M., et al. (2002). Attachment and autonomy as predictors of the development of social skills and delinquency during midadolescence. *Journal of Consulting and Clinical Psychology, 70*(1), 56–66.

Allen, J. P., McElhaney, K. B., Kuperminc, G. P., & Jodl, K. M. (2004). Stability and change in attachment security across adolescence. *Child Development, 75*(6), 1792–1805.

Allen, J. P., McElhaney, K. B., Land, D. J., Kuperminc, G. P., Moore, C. W., O'Beirne-Kelly, H., et al. (2003). A secure base in adolescence: Markers of attachment security in the mother-adolescent relationship. *Child Development, 74*(1), 292–307.

Allen, J. P., Moore, C., Kuperminc, G., & Bell, K. (1998). Attachment and adolescent psychosocial functioning. *Child Development, 69*(5), 1406–1419.

Ammaniti, M., van IJzendoorn, M. H., Speranza, A. M., & Tambelli, R. (2000). Internal working models of attachment during late childhood and early adolescence: An exploration of stability and change. *Attachment and Human Development, 2*(3), 328–346.

Arnett, J. J. (2000). Emerging adulthood: A theory of development from the late teens through the twenties. *American Psychologist, 55*(5), 469–480.

Bretherton, I. (1985). Attachment theory: Retrospect and prospect. *Monographs of the Society for Research in Child Development, 50*(1–2, Serial No. 209), 3–35.

Bretherton, I., & Munholland, K. A. (1999). Internal working models in attachment relationships: A construct revisited. In J. Cassidy & P. R. Shaver (Eds.), *Handbook of attachment: Theory, research and clinical applications* (pp. 89–111). New York: Guilford Press.

Carlivati, J. (2006). *Clarifying adolescent and adult attachment: Construct validation and establishment of associations between two relationship representations.* Unpublished doctoral dissertation, University of Minnesota.

Carlson, E. A., Jacobvitz, D., & Sroufe, L. A. (1995). A developmental investigation of inattentiveness and hyperactivity. *Child Development, 66,* 37–54.

Carlson, E. A., Sroufe, L. A., & Egeland, B. (2004). The construction of experience: A longitudinal study of representation and behavior. *Child Development, 75*(1), 66–83.

Cassidy, J. (1999). The nature of the child's ties. In J. Cassidy & P. R. Shaver (Eds.), *Handbook of attachment: Theory, research, and clinical applications* (pp. 3–20). New York: Guilford Press.

Cassidy, J. (2001). Truth, lies, and intimacy: An attachment perspective. *Attachment and Human Development, 3*(2), 121–155.

Collins, N. L., & Read, S. J. (1990). Adult attachment, working models, and relationship quality in dating couples. *Journal of Personality and Social Psychology, 58*(4), 644–663.

Collins, W. A. (1995). Relationships and development: Family adaptation to individual change. In S. Shulman (Ed.), *Close relationships and socioemotional development* (pp. 128–154). Norwood, NJ: Ablex.

Collins, W. A. (1997). Relationships and development during adolescence: Interpersonal adaptation to individual change. *Personal Relationships, 4,* 1–14.

Collins, W. A., & Sroufe, L. A. (1999). Capacity for intimate relationships: A developmental construction. In W. Furman, C. Feiring, & B. Brown (Eds.), *Contemporary perspectives on adolescent romantic relationships* (pp. 125–147). Cambridge: Cambridge University Press.

Crowell, J. A., Fraley, R. C., & Shaver, P. R. (1999). Measurement of individual differences in adolescent and adult attachment. In J. Cassidy & P. R. Shaver (Eds.), *Handbook of attachment: Theory, research, and clinical applications* (pp. 434–465). New York: Guilford Press.

Crowell, J. A., & Owens, G. (1996). *Current Relationship Interview and scoring system, Version 2.* Unpublished manuscript, State University of New York at Stony Brook.

Furman, W., & Buhrmester, D. (1992). Age and sex differences in perceptions of networks of personal relationships. *Child Development, 63,* 103–115.

Furman, W., & Simon, V. A. (1999). Cognitive representations of adolescent romantic relationships. In W. Furman, B. Brown, & C. Feiring (Eds.), *The development of romantic relationships in adolescence* (pp. 75–98). Cambridge: Cambridge University Press.

George, C., Kaplan, N., & Main, M. (1985). *An Adult Attachment Interview: Interview protocol.* Unpublished manuscript, University of California at Berkeley.

Griffin, D. W., & Bartholomew, K. (1994). Models of the self and other: Fundamental dimensions underlying measures of adult attachment. *Journal of Personality and Social Psychology, 67*(3), 430–445.

Hamilton, C. E. (2000). Continuity and discontinuity of attachment from infancy through adolescence. *Child Development, 71*(3), 690–694.

Helsen, M., Vollebergh, W., & Meeus, W. (2000). Social support from parents and friends and emotional problems in adolescence. *Journal of Youth and Adolescence, 29*(3), 319–335.

Hunter, F. T., & Youniss, J. (1982). Changes in the functions of three relations during adolescence. *Developmental Psychology, 18*(6), 806–811.

Kobak, R. (1999). The emotional dynamics of disruptions in attachment relationships: Implications for theory, research, and clinical intervention. In J. Cassidy & P. R. Shaver (Eds.), *Handbook of attachment: Theory, research and clinical applications* (pp. 21–43). New York: Guilford Press.

Kobak, R. R., & Sceery, A. (1988). Attachment in late adolescence: Working models, affect regulation, and representations of self and others. *Child Development, 59*(1), 135–146.

Laursen, B., Coy, K. C., & Collins, W. A. (1998). Reconsidering changes in parent-child conflict across adolescence: A meta-analysis. *Child Development, 69*(3), 817–832.

Lewis, M., Feiring, C., & Rosenthal, S. (2000). Attachment over time. *Child Development, 7*(3), 707–720.

Main, M., Kaplan, N., & Cassidy, J. (1985). Security in infancy, childhood, and adulthood: A move to the level of representation. *Monograph of the Society for Research in Child Development, 50* (1–2, Serial No. 209), 66–104.

Mayseless, O. (2004). Home leaving to military service: Attachment concerns, transfer of attachment functions from parents to peers, and adjustment. *Journal of Adolescent Research, 19*(5), 533–558.

Owens, G., Crowell, J. A., Pan, H., Treboux, D., O'Conner, E., & Waters, E. (1995). The prototype hypothesis and the origins of attachment working models: Adult relationships with parents and romantic partners. *Monographs of the Society for Research in Child Development, 60* (2–3, Serial No. 244), 216–233.

Reis, H. T., Collins, W. A., & Berscheid, E. (2000). Relationships in human behavior and development. *Psychological Bulletin, 126,* 844–872.

Roisman, G. I., Collins, W. A., Sroufe, L. A., & Egeland, B. (2005). Predictors of young adults' representations of and behavior in their current romantic relationship: Prospective tests of the prototype hypothesis. *Attachment and Human Development, 7*(2), 105–121.

Roisman, G. I., Madsen, S. D., Hennighausen, K. H., Sroufe, L. A., & Collins, W. A. (2001). The coherence of dyadic behavior across parent-child and romantic relationships as mediated by the internalized representation of experience. *Attachment and Human Development, 3*(2), 156–172.

Sampson, M. (2003, April). *Examining early correlates of self-report measures of adult attachment: A prospective longitudinal view.* Poster presented at the biennial meeting of the Society of Research in Child Development, Tampa, FL.

Sampson, M. C. (2004). *Continuity and change in patterns of attachment between infancy, adolescence, and early adulthood in a high risk sample.* Unpublished doctoral dissertation, University of Minnesota.

Sampson, M. C., & Carlson, E. A. (2005, April). *Prospective and concurrent correlates of attachment insecurity in young adulthood in a high risk sample.* Paper presented at the biennial meeting of the Society for Research in Child Development, Atlanta, GA.

Scharf, M., & Mayseless, O. (2005, April). *Away from home: Adolescents' attachment representations and adaptation to the leaving-home transition.* Paper presented at the biennial meeting of the Society for Research in Child Development, Atlanta, GA.

Scharf, M., Mayseless, O., & Kivenson-Baron, I. (2004). Adolescent attachment representations and developmental tasks in emerging adulthood. *Developmental Psychology, 40*(3), 430–444.

Scholte, R.H.J., van Lieshout, C.F.M., & van Aken, M.A.G. (2001). Perceived relational support in adolescence: Dimensions, configuration, and adolescent adjustment. *Journal of Research on Adolescence, 11*(1), 71–94.

Scott Brown, L., & Wright, J. (2003). The relationship between attachment strategies and psychopathology in adolescence. *Psychology and Psychotherapy: Theory, Research and Practice, 76*(4), 351–367.

Sroufe, L. A., Carlson, E., & Shulman, S. (1993). Individuals in relationships: Development from infancy through adolescence. In D. C. Funder, R. D. Parke, C. Tomlinson, & K. Widaman (Eds.). *Studying lives through time: Personality and development* (pp. 315–342). Washington, DC: American Psychological Association.

Sroufe, L. A., Egeland, B., Carlson, E. A., & Collins, W. A. (2005a). *The development of the person: The Minnesota Study of Risk and Adaptation from Birth to Adulthood.* New York: Guilford Press.

Sroufe, L. A., Egeland, B., Carlson, E. A., & Collins, W. A. (2005b). Placing early attachment experiences in developmental context: The Minnesota longitudinal study. In K. E. Grossmann, K. Grossmann, & E. Waters (Eds.), *Attachment from infancy to adulthood: The major longitudinal studies* (pp. 48–70). New York: Guilford Press.

Sroufe, L. A., & Fleeson, J. (1986). Attachment and the construction of relationships. In W. W. Hartup & Z. Rubin (Eds.), *Relationships and development* (pp. 51–71). Mahwah, NJ: Erlbaum.

Thompson, R. A. (2000). The legacy of early attachments. *Child Development, 71,* 145–152.

Treboux, D., Crowell, J. A., & Waters, E. (2004). When "new" meets "old": Configurations of adult attachment representations and their implications for marital functioning. *Developmental Psychology, 40*(2), 295–314.

van IJzendoorn, M. H., & Bakermans-Kranenburg, M. J. (1996). Attachment representations in mothers, fathers, adolescents, and clinical groups: A meta-analytic search for normative data. *Journal of Consulting and Clinical Psychology, 64*(1), 8–21.

Waters, E., & Cummings, E. M. (2000). A secure base from which to explore close relationships. *Child Development, 71*(1), 164–172.

Waters, E., Hamilton, C. E., & Weinfield, N. S. (2000). The stability of attachment security from infancy to adolescence and early adulthood: General introduction. *Child Development, 71*(3), 678–683.

Waters, E., Kondo-Ikemura, K., Posada, G., & Richters, J. E. (1991). Learning to love: Mechanisms and milestones. In M. R. Gunnar & L. A. Sroufe (Eds.), *Self processes and development* (pp. 217–255). Mahwah, NJ: Erlbaum.

Waters, E., Merrick, S., Treboux, D., Crowell, J., & Albersheim, L. (2000). Attachment security in infancy and early adulthood: A twenty-year longitudinal study. *Child Development, 71*(3), 684–689.

Waters, E., Weinfield, N. S., & Hamilton, C. E. (2000). The stability of attachment security from infancy to adolescence and early adulthood: General discussion. *Child Development, 71*(3), 703–706.

Weinfield, N. S., Sroufe, L. A., & Egeland, B. (2000). Attachment from infancy to early adulthood in a high-risk sample: Continuity, discontinuity, and their correlates. *Child Development, 71*(3), 695–702.

Weinfield, N. S., Sroufe, L. A., Egeland, B., & Carlson, E. A. (1999). The nature of individual differences in infant-caregiver attachment. In J. Cassidy & P. R. Shaver (Eds.), *Handbook of attachment: Theory, research, and clinical applications* (pp. 68–88). New York: Guilford Press.

Weinfield, N. S., Whaley, G.J.L., & Egeland, B. (2004). Continuity, discontinuity, and coherence in attachment from infancy to late adolescence: Sequelae of organization and disorganization. *Attachment and Human Development, 6*(1), 73–97.

Yates, T. M., Egeland, B., & Sroufe, L. A. (2003). Rethinking resilience: A developmental process perspective. In S. S. Luthar (Ed.), *Resilience and vulnerabilities: Adaptation in the context of childhood adversities* (pp. 243–266). Cambridge: Cambridge University Press.

Zimmermann, P. (2004). Attachment representation and characteristics of friendship relations during adolescence. *Journal of Experimental Child Psychology, 88*(1), 83–101.

Zimmermann, P., Maier, M. A., Winter, M., & Grossmann, K. E. (2001). Attachment and adolescents' emotion regulation during a joint problem-solving task with a friend. *International Journal of Behavioral Development, 25*(4), 331–343.

JILL CARLIVATI *is a visiting assistant professor at the George Washington University, Washington, D.C.*

W. ANDREW COLLINS *is Morse-Alumni Distinguished Teaching Professor of Child Development at the University of Minnesota, Minneapolis.*

INDEX

Is this disturbing trend a worldwide problem? To answer this question, we must begin to study the developmental and cultural origins of respect and disrespect. Five research teams report that respect and disrespect are influenced by experiences in the family, school, community, and, most importantly, the broader cultural setting. The chapters introduce a new topic area for mainstream developmental sciences that is relevant to the interests of scholars, educators, practitioners, and policymakers.
ISBN 978-07879-95584

CAD 113 **The Modernization of Youth Transitions in Europe**
Manuela du Bois-Reymond, Lynne Chisholm, Editors
This compelling volume focuses on what it is like to be young in the rapidly changing, enormously diverse world region that is early 21st century Europe. Designed for a North American readership interested in youth and young adulthood, *The Modernization of Youth Transitions in Europe* provides a rich fund of theoretical insight and empirical evidence about the implications of contemporary modernization processes for young people living, learning, and working across Europe. Chapters have been specially written for this volume by well-known youth sociologists; they cover a wide range of themes against a shared background of the reshaping of the life course and its constituent phases toward greater openness and contigency. New modes of learning accompany complex routes into employment and career under rapidly changing labor market conditions and occupational profiles, while at the same time new family and lifestyle forms are developing alongside greater intergenerational responsibilities in the face of the retreat of the modern welfare state. The complex patterns of change for today's young Europeans are set into a broader framework that analyzes the emergence and character of European youth research and youth policy in recent years.
ISBN 978-07879-88890

CAD 112 **Rethinking Positive Adolescent Female Sexual Development**
Lisa M. Diamond, Editor
This volume provides thoughtful and diverse perspectives on female adolescent sexuality. These perspectives integrate biological, cultural, and interpersonal influences on adolescent girls' sexuality, and highlight the importance of using multiple methods to investigate sexual ideation and experience. Traditional portrayals cast adolescent females as sexual gatekeepers whose primary task is to fend off boys' sexual overtures and set aside their own sexual desires in order to reduce their risks for pregnancy and sexually transmitted diseases. Yet an increasing number of thoughtful and constructive critiques have challenged this perspective, arguing for more sensitive, in-depth, multimethod investigations into the positive meanings of sexuality for adolescent girls that will allow us to conceptualize (and, ideally, advocate for) healthy sexual-developmental trajectories. Collectively, authors of this volume take up this movement and chart exciting new directions for the next generation of developmental research on adolescent female sexuality.
ISBN 978-07879-87350

CAD111 **Family Mealtime as a Context for Development and Socialization**
Reed W. Larson, Angela R. Wiley, Kathryn R. Branscomb, Editors
This issue examines the impact of family mealtime on the psychological development of young people. In the popular media, family mealtime is often presented as a vital institution for the socialization and development of young people, but also as one that is "going the way of the dinosaur." Although elements such as fast food and TV have become a part of many family mealtimes, evidence is beginning to suggest that mealtimes can also provide rich oppor-

tunities for children's and adolescents' development. While what happens at mealtimes varies greatly among families, an outline of the forms and functions of mealtimes is beginning to emerge from this research. In this issue, leading mealtime researchers from the fields of history, cultural anthropology, psycholinguistics, psychology, and nutrition critically review findings from each of their disciplines, giving primary focus on family mealtimes in the United States. The authors in this issue examine the history of family mealtimes, describe contemporary mealtime practices, elucidate the differing transactional processes that occur, and evaluate evidence on the outcomes associated with family mealtimes from children and adolescents.
ISBN 978-07879-85776

CAD 110 **Leaks in the Pipeline to Math, Science, and Technology Careers**
Janis E. Jacobs, Sandra D. Simpkins, Editors
Around the world, the need for highly trained scientists and technicians remains high, especially for positions that require employees to have a college degree and skills in math, science, and technology. The pipeline into these jobs begins in high school, but many "leaks" occur before young people reach the highly educated workforce needed to sustain leadership in science and technology. Students drop out of the educational pipeline in science and technology at alarming rates at each educational transition beginning in high school, but women and ethnic minority youth drop out at a faster rate. Women and minorities are consistently underrepresented in science and engineering courses and majors. They account for a small portion of the work force in high-paying and more innovative jobs that require advanced degrees. This schism between the skills necessary in our ever-changing economy and the skill set that most young adults acquire is troubling. It leads us to ask the question that forms the basis for this issue. Why are adolescents and young adults, particularly women and minorities, opting out of the math, science, and technology pipeline? The volume addresses gender and ethnic differences in the math, science, and technology pipeline from multiple approaches, including theoretical perspectives, a review of the work in this field, presentation of findings from four longitudinal studies, and a discussion of research implications given the current educational and economic climate.
ISBN 978-07879-83932

CAD 109 **New Horizons in Developmental Theory and Research**
Lene Arnett Jensen, Reed W. Larson, Editors
This inaugural issue by the new editors-in-chief brings together a group of cutting-edge developmental scholars who each report on promising new lines of theory and research within their specialty areas. Their essays cover a selection of important topics including emotion-regulation, family socialization, friendship, self, civic engagement, media, and culture. In the succinct, engaging essays, all authors provide thought-provoking views of the horizons in the field.
ISBN 978-07879-83413

CAD 108 **Changing Boundaries of Parental Authority During Adolescence**
Judith Smetena, Editor
This volume describes research focusing on changes in different dimensions of parenting and conceptions of parental authority during adolescence. The seven chapters illuminate the dimensions of parenting that change (or remain stable) over the course of adolescence. The chapters also ighlight the importance of considering variations in parenting accoding to the different domains of adolescents' lives, their relationships to the development of responsibility automony, and how these are influenced by socioeconomic status, culture,

and ethnicity. Thus, the chapters in this volume provide new directions for conceptualizing variations in parenting over the second decade of life and their implicaions for adolescent adjustment and well-being. The authors point to the need for developmentally sensitive models of parenting that consider changes within domains over time, their influence on adolescent development and functioning, and potential asynchronies between parents and adolescents.
ISBN 978-07879-81921

CAD 107 **The Experience of Close Friendship in Adolescence**
Niobe Way, Jill V. Hamm, Editors
In this issue, we present findings from four studies that employed qualitative methodology to gain insight into the how and the why of close friendships. How do adolescents experience trust and intimacy in their friendships? Why are these relational experiences critical for emotional adjustment? And how does the social and cultural context shape the ways in which adolescents experience their close friendships? The studies reveal the ways in which adolescents from diverse cultural backgrounds speak about their close friendships and the individual and contextual factors that shape and are shaped by their experiences of close friendships.
ISBN 978-07879-80573

CAD 106 **Social and Self Process Underlying Math and Science Achievement**
Heather Bouchey, Cynthia Winston, Editors
In general, America's students are not faring well in science and mathematics. The chapters in this volume employ novel conceptual and empirical approaches to investigate how social and individual factors interact to effect successful math and science achievement. Each of the chapters is solidly grounded in theory and provides new insight concerning the integration of student-level and contextual influences. Inclusion of youth from diverse socioeconomic and ethnic backgrounds is a salient feature of the volume.
ISBN 978-07879-79164

CAD 105 **Human Technogenesis: Cultural Pathways Through the Information Age**
Dinesh Sharma, Editor
The technologically driven information economy is reshaping everyday human behavior and sociocultural environments. Yet our paradigms for understanding human development within a cultural framework are guided by traditional and dichotomous ideas about the social world (for example, individualism-collectivism, egocentric-sociocentric, modern-traditional, Western-Non-Western). As the impact of information technologies permeates all aspects of our lives, research in human development and psychology must face the digitally, connected social environments as its laboratory, filled with naturally occurring experiments, whether it is the speed at which we now communicate in the home or workplace, the far-reaching access children have to a wide array of information previously unavailable, or the vicarious anonymity with which we are able to participate in each other's lives through the new media tools. The chapters in this volume claim that the recent wave of innovation and adaptation to information technologies, giving rise to a new form of "human technogenesis," is fundamentally transforming our everyday interactions and potentially reconstructing the nature and process of human development. Human technogenesis is the constructive process of individual and sociocultural innovation and adaptation to the everyday interactions with information technologies, which significantly affects the developing and the developed mind.
ISBN 978-07879-77795

developmental impact. Both distal (for example, attachment styles with parents, community violence exposure) and proximal (for example, perceptions of enemies' behavior, social structure of the peer group) factors related to inimical relations are explored, and the developmental sequelaw (for example, affective, behavioral, interpersonal) of having enemies are examined with concurrent and longitudinal designs.
ISBN 978-07879-72721

CAD 101 **Person-Centered Approaches to Studying Development in Context**
Stephen C. Peck, Robert W. Roeser, Editors
This volume introduces readers to theoretical and methodological discussions, along with empirical illustrations, of using pattern-centered analyses in studying development in context. Pattern-centered analytic techniques refer to a family of research tools that identify patterns or profiles of variables within individuals and thereby classify individuals into homogeneous subgroups based on their similarity of profile. These techniques find their theoretical foundation in holistic, developmental systems theories in which notions of organization, process dynamics, interactions and transactions, context, and life course development are focal. The term *person-centered* is used to contrast with the traditional emphasis on variables; the term *pattern-centered* is used to extend the principles of person-centered approaches to other levels of analysis (for example, social context). Contributors present the theoretical foundations of pattern-centered analytic techniques, describe specific tools that may be of use to developmentalists interested in using such techniques and provide four empirical illustrations of their use in relation to educational achievement and attainments, aggressive behavior and social popularity, and alcohol use during the childhood and adolescent periods.
ISBN 978-07879-71694

CAD 100 **Exploring Cultural Conceptions of the Transitions to Adulthood**
Jeffrey Jensen Arnett, Editor
The transition to adulthood has been studied for decades in terms of transition events such as leaving home, finishing education, and entering marriage and parenthood, but only recently have studies examined the conceptions of young people themselves on what it means to become an adult. The goal of this volume is to extend the study of conceptions of adulthood to a wider range of cultures. The chapters in this volume examine conceptions of adulthood among Israelis, Argentines, American Mormons, Germans, Canadians, and three American ethnic minority groups. There is a widespread emphasis across cultures on individualistic criteria for adulthood, but each culture has been found to emphasize culturally distinctive criteria as well. This volume represents a beginning in research on cultural conceptions of the transition to adulthood and points the way to a broad range of opportunities for future investigation.
ISBN 978-07879-69813

CAD 99 **Examining Adolescent Leisure Time Across Cultures: Developmental Opportunities and Risks**
Suman Verma, Reed W. Larson, Editors
Adolescence worldwide is a life period of role restructuring and social learning. Free-time activities provide opportunities to experiment with roles and develop new adaptive strategies and other interpersonal skills that have an impact on development, socialization, and the transition to adulthood. Leisure provides a rich context in which adolescents can gain control over

their attentional processes and learn from relationships with peers, but it also has potential costs, such as involvement in deviant and risk behaviors. To gain deeper insight into the developmental opportunities and risks that adolescents experience in their free time, this volume explores adolescents' daily leisure experience across countries. Each chapter describes the sociocultural contexts in which adolescents live, along with a profile of free-time activities. Collectively, the chapters highlight the differences and similarities between cultures; how family, peers, and wider social factors influence the use of free time; which societies provide more freedom and at what costs; and how adolescents cope with restricted degrees of freedom and with what consequences on their mental health and well-being.

ISBN 978-07879-68366

New Directions for Child & Adolescent Development
Order Form
SUBSCRIPTIONS AND SINGLE ISSUES

DISCOUNTED BACK ISSUES:

Use this form to receive **20% off** all back issues of New Directions for Child & Adolescent Development . All single issues priced at **$23.20** (normally $29.00)

TITLE	ISSUE NO.	ISBN
_____	_____	_____
_____	_____	_____
_____	_____	_____

Call 888-378-2537 or see mailing instructions below. When calling, mention the promotional code, JB7ND, to receive your discount.
For a complete list of issues, please visit www.josseybass.com/go/ndcad

SUBSCRIPTIONS: (1 year, 4 issues)

☐ New Order   ☐ Renewal

U.S.	☐ Individual: $85	☐ Institutional: $258
Canada/Mexico	☐ Individual: $85	☐ Institutional: $298
All Others	☐ Individual: $109	☐ Institutional: $332

Call 888-378-2537 or see mailing and pricing instructions below. Online subscriptions are available at www.interscience.wiley.com.

Copy or detach page and send to:
**John Wiley & Sons, Journals Dept, 5th Floor
989 Market Street, San Francisco, CA 94103-1741**

Order Form can also be faxed to: 888-481-2665

	SHIPPING CHARGES:		
Issue/Subscription Amount: $ _____			
Shipping Amount: $ _____	SURFACE	Domestic	Canadian
(for single issues only—subscription prices include shipping)	First Item	$5.00	$6.00
Total Amount: $ _____	Each Add'l Item	$3.00	$1.50

(No sales tax for U.S. subscriptions. Canadian residents, add GST for subscription orders. Individual rate subscriptions must be paid by personal check or credit card. Individual rate subscriptions may not be resold as library copies.)

☐ Payment enclosed (U.S. check or money order only. All payments must be in U.S. dollars.)

☐ VISA ☐ MC ☐ Amex # _____ Exp. Date _____

Card Holder Name _____ Card Issue # _____

Signature_____ Day Phone _____

☐ Bill Me (U.S. institutional orders only. Purchase order required.)

Purchase order # _____
Federal Tax ID13559302   GST 89102 8052

Name_____

Address _____

Phone _____ E-mail _____

JB7ND

NEW DIRECTIONS FOR
CHILD AND ADOLESCENT DEVELOPMENT
IS NOW AVAILABLE ONLINE AT WILEY INTERSCIENCE

What is Wiley InterScience?

Wiley InterScience is the dynamic online content service from John Wiley & Sons delivering the full text of over 300 leading scientific, technical, medical, and professional journals, plus major reference works, the acclaimed Current Protocols laboratory manuals, and even the full text of select Wiley print books online.

What are some special features of Wiley InterScience?

Wiley Interscience Alerts is a service that delivers table of contents via e-mail for any journal available on Wiley InterScience as soon as a new issue is published online.
EarlyView is Wiley's exclusive service presenting individual articles online as soon as they are ready, even before the release of the compiled print issue. These articles are complete, peer-reviewed, and citable.
CrossRef is the innovative multi-publisher reference linking system enabling readers to move seamlessly from a reference in a journal article to the cited publication, typically located on a different server and published by a different publisher.

How can I access Wiley InterScience?

Visit http://www.interscience.wiley.com.

Guest Users can browse Wiley InterScience for unrestricted access to journal tables of contents and article abstracts, or use the powerful search engine.
Registered Users are provided with a *Personal Home Page* to store and manage customized alerts, searches, and links to favorite journals and articles. Additionally, Registered Users can view free online sample issues and preview selected material from major reference works.
Licensed Customers are entitled to access full-text journal articles in PDF, with select journals also offering full-text HTML.

How do I become an Authorized User?

Authorized Users are individuals authorized by a paying Customer to have access to the journals in Wiley InterScience. For example, a university that subscribes to Wiley journals is considered to be the Customer.
Faculty, staff, and students authorized by the university to have access to those journals in Wiley InterScience are Authorized Users. Users should contact their library for information on which Wiley journals they have access to in Wiley InterScience.